Best Practices in Academic Libraries

Best Practices in Academic Libraries

Editor

Shilpa Satish Waghchoure

Ess Ess Publications
New Delhi

BEST PRACTICES IN ACADEMIC LIBRARIES

ISBN: 978-81-7000-775-3

First Published 2016

Published by:
Ess Ess Publications
4831/24, Ansari Road,
Darya Ganj,
New Delhi-110 002.
INDIA
Phones: 23260807, 41563444
Fax: 41563334
E-mail: info@essessreference.com
www.essessreference.com

Cover Design by *Patch Creative Unit*

Printed and bound in India at Salasar Imaging Systems.

Contents

Preface

List of Contributors

1. Best Practices: A Case Study of Rayat Shikshan Sanstha's Ycis Satara Library 1
   Amol Dewaji Khobragade
2. Best Practices of Pcacs Learning Resource Centre, New Panvel 10
   Sanjay B. Munavalli
3. Innovative Services in Sardar Vallabhabhai Patel Arts and Science College Ainpur (SVPCA) Library 23
   Rahul B. Khandare
   Shashank S. Sonwane
4. Best Practices of Chetana's H. S. College of Commerce & Economics and Smt. Kusumati Chaudhri College of Art, Bandra 34
   Sanjay Narayan More
   Kusumati Chaudhri
5. Best Practices in Library of R.N.C. Arts, J.D.B. Commerce And N.S.C. Science College, Nashik Road 45
   Ravindra B. Bagul

6. Best Practices in Academic College Libraries With Reference to BMCC Library 50
Damodar Dasharath Waghmare

7. Best Practices of Chandmal Tarachand Bora College Library & Information Centre 67
Shantashree Sengupta

8. Best Practices in the Library : A Case Study of DGT College Library 82
Jagdish Vyas
Dahifale Vikram

9. Best Practices in Ness Wadia College of Commerce Library Pune 94
Manojkumar Thakur
Surekha R. Khare

10. Best Practices of Dr. T.K.Tope Arts & Commerce Night Senior College, Parel, Mumbai 103
Nandu Sahebrao More

11. Best Practices at Maeer's Mitsom Library 109
Nitin S Joshi

12. Best Practices of Gandhi Shikshan Bhavan's, Smt. Surajaba College of Education 127
Pradnya Anil Bhosekar

13. Best Practices in Library of Nirmala Niketan College of Home Science, Mumbai 130
Prajakata P. Mhaprolkar

14. Generating "Best Practices" to Galvanize the Quality in Academic Libraries 142
Pratibha. A. Kanojia

15. Best Practices in Academic Libraries : A Case Study of Bhurani College of Commerce & Arts, Mazgaon, Mumbai 149
Sujata Sunil Rajpurkar

16. Best Practices of SMRK-BK-AK Mahila Mahavidyalaya, Library, Nashik 155
S. A. Kulkarni

17. User Centric Best Practices of Khandwala College Library 161
Santosh C. Hulagabali

18. ICT Based Best Practices & Innovations in Chhatrapati Shahu Ji Maharaj Centre for Studies of Maratha History Library 174
Kamble Ashwini Rajarm

19. Best Practices in Academic Libraries with Special Reference to the Chakdaha College Library, Nadia, West Bengal: An Empirical Study 182
Ranjan Karmakar

20. Best Practices in Shri M. D. Shah Mahila College of Arts and Commerce, College Library, Malad, Mumbai 214
Vinay P. Haware

21. Open Study Centre as A Best Practices at Mss's, Arts, Science and Commerce College Library, Ambad, Jalna 222
Shivshankar Ghumre

22. Best Practices in Academic Libraries Prescribed by NAAC 227
Shilpa Satish Waghchoure

DR. BABASAHEB AMBEDKAR MARATHWADA UNIVERSITY, AURANGABAD 431 004

UNIVERSITY LIBRARY
(NAAC REACCREDITED A)

Dr. D. K. Veer,
M.Com, M.Lib.Sc, Ph.D
Librarian
Tel. No. (Office) : (0240) 2403190 To 2403194
Fax No. : (0240) 2403190
Web Site: www.bamu.net
E-mail : dharmaraj.veer@gmail.com

University Campus
Aurangabad 431 004
(Maharashtra)

FOREWORD

The Present Information and Communication Technologies (ICT) have made a tremendous impact on the functions of the academic libraries. The developments and changes in the ICT have changed the user's expectations from the academic libraries in different ways. The ways to build a library collection and offer services to the end users vary from the recent to past exercises. Thus to effectively meet the demands of the end users, the academic libraries need to identify and adopt good and best practices and benchmarks which will ultimately enhance the value based services of the libraries in an academic environment.

The role of the library and information centre in the college is aimed at realizing the educational goals of the college or the parent organization. The Academic Libraries not only provides stimulus to reading by procuring materials for study and research, by introducing open access system, by providing long hours of open, by organizing the library resources in a systematic way, but also feeds the intellect of the student, encourage the researches of the faculty and thus serve the teaching and research needs of the faculty. The academic library and information resource centre acts as a vehicle for disseminating information and the related computer technologies through the best practices for utilization by its community of users and also for the exchange of information among its users.

This Edited Volume is one such mechanism to take stock of the best practices in Academic Libraries. It is matter of great satisfaction that there is tremendous response to this edited book. Out of received papers 22 have been selected for inclusion in volume which is presented in the form of book entitled, **"Best Practices in Academic Libraries"**.

I am eagerly looking forward to the learned outcomes and valuable recommendations of this edited volume. I really appreciated to the Editor **Dr. Shilpa S Waghchoure** who has taken sincere efforts for editing beautiful & informative book.

Dr. D. K. Veer
University Librarian
Dr.B.A.M.U Aurangabad

Preface

Library and Information System Management is the basic and core activity which helps the user community in identifying and accessing knowledge resources in an academic institution.

It also comprises the activities performed in relation to the development of vision, mission, goals and policies of the library, working hours, stock verification methods, copyright issues, membership, budgeting and reporting, resource mobilization, technical processing methods, manpower development, basic amenities and facilities as well as collection development management or information resources development, technical services, information services generation, technological, legal and copy right issues, to name a few. It also concerns with strategic planning of LIS in present and future operations. Identifying and internalization of best practices in the management and administrative functions at regular interval would enhance the collection development process, services dissemination and use of the library as a whole. Active participation and periodic meetings of library advisory committee, involvement of librarian in academic activities of the college/university, support from the management, participation of the users, standard facilities with innovative library buildings, regular flow of resource generation, skilled and qualified staff deployment with further training, capacity building in terms of information and communication technology, information dissemination facilities etc. are a few areas where best practices can be accommodated. Appropriate planning and fore thinking is required in attaining the above mentioned with a detailed analysis of user base, objectives of the affiliating institution and its future strategies. As the management and administration of the library is pivotal in collection development and delivery of information products and services to the end users, adoption of best practices in this area lead to continuous improvement in overall performance.

The edited book 'BEST PRACTICES IN ACADEMIC LIBRARIES' is an attempt to compile the case studies of the best practices used by the contributors at their libraries. Total 21 case studies has been presented in this book from various institutions.

This book will definitely help to the library professional who will go for NAAC accreditation in their institutions. They can collect the new practices from the book and will try to implement to their respective institutions.

Shilpa Satish Waghchoure

List of Contributors

Amol Dewaji Khobragade
Librarian/ Co-ordinator
YCMOU, YCIS Satara.
amolk2410@gmail.com

Dahifale Vikram
R.M.I.G.College , Jalna.
vdahifale@gmail.com

Damodar Dasharath Waghmare
Librarian
Willingdon College Sangli.
damodarwaghmare@gmail.com

Jagdish Vyas
Research Scholar
SRTMU, Nanded
jrvyas5@gmail.com

Kamble Ashwini Rajarm
Librarian, Shri Shivajirao Deshmukh
College of Education, Red-Shirala.
Tal-Shirala Dist-Sangli
kamble.ash25@gmail.com

Rahul B. Khandare
Librarian
S.V.P. Arts & Science College,
Ainpur, Tal. Raver, Dist. Jalgaon (M.S.)- 425507
rahulkhandare39@yahoo.in

Ravindra B. Bagul
Librarian
R. N. C. Arts. J. D. B. Commerce & N. S. C. Science College
Nashik Road.
ravindrabagul4467@gmail.com

Manojkumar Thakur
Librarian
M.Com. M.Lib. & I. Sc., SET
manojkumart671@gmail.com

Nandu Sahebrao More
Librarian
Dr.T.K.Tope Arts & Commerce
Night Senior College, Parel, Mumbai.

Nitin S Joshi
Librarian
MAEER's MIT School of Management,
Pune (Maharashtra)
nitinjoshi@mitsom.com

Pradnya Anil Bhosekar
Librarian, Gandhi Shikshan Bhavan's,
Smt. Surajaba College of Education
Juhu Road (north), Juhu Mumbai 400049.
pradnyaanil@rediffmail.com

Prajakata P. Mhaprolkar
Librarian, Nirmala Niketan college of Home Science
49, New Marine Lines, Mumbai 400020.
pmhaprolkar@gmail.com

Pratibha.A. Kanojia
Librarian, Secondary Training College
3, Mahapalika Marg, Dhobi Talao, Mumbai-400001.
pratibha_kanojia@rediffmail.com

Ranjan Karmakar
College Librarian,
Chakdaha College, Chakdaha, Nadia – 741222,
West Bengal.
ranjankarmakar01@gmail.com

Sanjay Narayan More
Chetana's H.S. College of Commerce & Economics and
Smt. Kusumati Chaudhri College of Art
Bandra (E) Mumbai 400051.
sanjaymore.more@gmail.com

Sanjay B. Munavalli
Librarian, Pillai College of Arts,Commerce & Science
New Panvel-410206
sbmunavalli@gmail.com

Santosh C. Hulagabali
Librarian, Nagindas Khandwala College,
Malad (W), Mumbai-400 064
santosh@nkc.ac.in

Shantashree Sengupta
Librarian & Head,
Department of Library & Information Science,
Chandmal Tarachand Bora Arts,
Commerce & Science College
Shirur, Dist.Pune.
shantashrees@gmail.com

Shashank S. Sonwane
Assistant Professor,
Dept. of Library and Information Science,
Dr. Babasaheb Ambedkar Marathwada
University, Aurangabad (M.S.) - 431004
shashank65@yahoo.com

(Mrs) Shilpa S. Waghchoure
Librarian, Gokhale Education Society's
College of Education and Research
Parel, Mumbai - 400 012.
sswaghchoure@gmail.com

Shivshankar Ghumre
Librarian, MSS's, Arts, Science and Commerce College,
Ambad Dist. Jalna
drskghumre@gmail.com

Sujata Sunil Rajpurkar
Librarian, Burhani College of Comm.
and Arts, Mazgaon, Mumbai.
sujukamble@rediffmail.com

Surekha R. Khare
Assistant Librarian
kharesurekha@gmail.com

S. A. Kulkarni
Librarian, Smrk-BK-AK Mahila Mahvidyalaya
Prin. T.A. Kulkarni Vidyanagar,
Nashik-422005.
sakulkarni1@gmail.com

Vinay P. Haware
Librarian
Shri. M.D.Shah Mahila College of Arts & Commerce,
B.J.Patel Road, Malad (W) Mumbai 64.
vinayhaware@gmail.com

1

Best Practices: A Case Study of Rayat Shikshan Sanstha's YCIS Satara Library

Amol Dewaji Khobragade
Librarian/Co-ordinator, YCMOU, YCIS Satara

ABSTRACT

A changingtrend in the mode of procurement, storage, processing and particularly in the delivery of services of the libraries is observed in almost all the libraries of the modern age. Also there are libraries continuing the traditional services and attempting towards provision of new services. In the changing scenario, ICT (Information and Communication Technology) has been the most instrumental factor. In this backdrop, in our paper, taking YCIS Sataralibrary, as a case study, an attempt has been made to highlight the innovative practices adopted in the mode of delivery of services.

Keywords : Library Services, Innovative Practices, Case Study.

INTRODUCTION

Library is considered as an important part of the college which is the major learning resource for the students and staff. As per the changing time, role of library is also being changed. Advanced technology has been utilized by the library to provide library services. The main aim of library is to avail the various reading material and learning resources to the students and work for the amusement and imbibe values in the readers by reading various autobiographies of great leaders. Students get inspirations and life-force for their future life by reading.

Library and information science (LIS) is a multi-disciplinary and dynamic field which adapts rapidly to technological and social developments, and keeps pace with emerging ideas and technologies. The willingness of library and information professionals to proactively accept changes and venture into new knowledge territories is helping the LIS discipline to stay relevant and useful in the fast changing society. Other factors that are driving innovation and creativity in LIS, are the popularity of the Web as an alternative source for information acquisition as well as competition from non-library agencies now involved in information provision.

Information and communication Technology (ICT) has been considered as the most instrumental factor for the change in the mode of delivery of library services.

General and traditional services of the library have been influenced with the introduction of new innovative practices, because of application of new ICT –based products and services.

2. RAYAT SHIKSHAN SANSTHA

Late Padmabhushan Dr. Karmaveer Bhaurao Patil founded Rayat Shikshan Sanstha in 1919 with a view to provide education to all classes of the society. "Education through self help" is our motto. Rayat Shikshan Sanstha is the biggest educational institution in Asia in a class of its own. It is spread over 14 districts of Maharashtra and 1 district of Karnataka having 674 branches which include colleges, industrial training institutes, high schools, primary and pre-primary schools and ashram shalas. At present it caters to the educational need of upto 4.5 lakh students through excellence human resource of 1800 workforce.

Karmaveer Vidhya Probodhini is the academic council of our institution involved in undertaking the projects indigenously to keep pace with the challenges in the competitive world.

2.1. YCIS Satara Institute

Yashavantrao Chavan Institute of Science started as science wing of Chh. Shivaji College Satara in 1958 and then developed as fully fledge independent single faculty science college in 1965. Later in 1968 it was renamed as "YashavantraoChavan Institute of Science" in the honour of former deputy prime minister, Late YashavantraoChavan. Accredited and reaccredited with A Grade by NAAC. Our institute is a place with a glorious past and boundless future. At Y.C.I.S. you can find tools, expertise and inspiration to make your ambitions a reality.

We pride ourselves on offering our students an excellent education and strive to provide an inspiring environment to encourage them by organizing state level

KarmaveerQuize Competition, Seminars, Projects, Personality Development Programmes, VidnyanManch, Competitive Exam Guidance Centre, Youth Festival, Sports etc. Extension activities are strenghthened through N.S.S. and N.C.C. Highly qualified devoted and dedicated faculty is our strength. We have recognized post graduate courses in Botany, Chemistry, Microbiology, Physics, Statistics and Zoology. Institute imparts quality education to more than 5000 students not only by offering a variety of U.G. and P.G. courses but also research programmes.

2.2. YCIS Satara Library

The institute has well equipped up-to-date library with varieties of books. More than 63637 Textbooks and Reference books are available in the library. Various periodicals of National and International repute have been available for the sake of all round development of students. 12 daily news papers of state and national level both in Marathi and English and 46 Magazines on various disciplines are subscribed.

Book Bank facility is an important part of the institute. Due to the rising cost of the books students are unable to purchase such books therefore book bank facility is provided to meet the reading thrust of the students. The library has made special study room facility for both students. They are taking benefit of this facility. The college has undertaken computerization of library with the help of MKCL's LIBRERIA software.

Library also effectively runs B.Lib and M.Lib courses under YCMOU, Nashik.

2.3.1. Building

The Library building situated near main building of the institute. The total area of the library is 17.52 Sq. mt.

2.3.2. Collection

The library collection is growing steadily covering

both in the form of published and unpublished materials. As on 31st March, 2013the collection of the library was as follows;

Total No. of Books	:	63637
Total No. of Journal Title	:	28
Newspapers	:	12
Magazines	:	18
E-journals	:	N-List
Other E-resources (CD, DVD etc.)	:	275
Theses/Dissertations	:	250

2.3.3. User Community

The teachers, research scholars (Ph.D. & M.Phil. students), PG students, UG students and non-teaching staff of the Institute are the regular members of the library. There are a total of about 2060 regular members of the library. Besides a number of visitors who are not registered are also visiting the library to avail the facilities. About 300 visitors visit the library daily.

2.3.4. Library Staff

The present staff positions of the library are as follows:

Librarian	:	1
Asst. Librarian	:	1
Library Clerk	:	2
Library Attendants	:	6
Other Casual staff	:	4

3. AUTOMATION STATUS

YCIS SataraLibrary initiated its automation process since 2009. We install "LIBRERIA" Library Software, developed by MKCL, Pune. The present automation status of the library is as follows:

- Creation of Database of Booksand new additions.
- Total database contains records of about 29,326 materials.
- About 9 computers for staff are used for automation work.
- Installation of OPAC (Online Public Access Catalogue);
- Installation of Bar code system in circulation system;
- Other Administrative aspects of the library.

4. YCIS SATARALIBRARY SERVICES

The teacher, research scholars (Ph.D. & M.Phil. students), students and the non-teaching staff are the main users of the library .The majority of the Post Graduate & undergraduate students of the Institute depend on the collection and the services of the library. For convenience of the readers, the service of the library is made available from 9AM to 6 PM on all working days. Reprographic services are provided to the readers on nominal charges to enable them to copy the required materials. The library provides Internet services to the readers for browsing the required materials.

4.1. General Services/ Facilities

The general services of the library include:

- General administrative works
- Procurement of information resources to serve the users;
- Infrastructure development in the tune of the demands of the users
- Issue and return of books, circulation of reference and journal materials and other materials for reading room service;
- Basic training on the handling of new services as a part of users education programme

- Reprographic services.
- Best Reader Award
- Book-bank Facility
- Scholar's Card
- Membership tonon-students
- Orators Card Facility
- Open Access Facility
- Stack arrangement and maintenance.

4.2. Traditional Services

The following traditional services have been prevailing in the library till date:

- Organization of Knowledge resources;
- Classification following DDC 19th Edition
- Circulation of reading materials;
- Reprographic Service;
- Reading Room Service;
- Reference Service;
- SMS Service
- E-mail Reference Service to the staff

4.3. Innovative Practices

From 2009 we are starting of automation workand create a blog through them new innovative practices have been introduced in the delivery of services by the library. Such practices can be summed up in the following ways:

- E-commerce and its application in the general administrative activities of the library with the use of new ICT enabled services, such as
  - — Contacting people, vendors, publishers, suppliers, etc.
  - — Submitting requirements of the holding to be procured electronically;

— Replacing manual clerical works by computers, etc.

- Automation of different house keeping operations of the library.
- Provision of services in electronic environment;
- Developing Local Area Network;
- Internet connectivity enabling the users access to global information resources;
- Joining the INFLIBNET N-LIST E:journal & E-Books enabling the academic and research community access foreign journals;
- Improving the efficiency and effectiveness of the library;
- Making library management more systematic to serve the users conductively;
- Changing towards overall development of the library.
- Adopting Barcode System in circulation system.

Currently, users of the YCIS SataraLibrary are getting in following Services:

- Access to the full text of the journals;
- Easy access to the journals;
- Assistant from the professionals to use the e-resources made available on N-LIST as well as our library blog.
- Provision of up to date information;
- Saving time in searching desired information;
- Fulfilling the need of the users;
- More information on career opportunities and jobs.

5. CONCLUSION

With the introduction of new innovative practices, the mode of delivery of services of library has really changed. The above mentioned description presents the situation in respect of YCISSatara Library. The new practices introduced by the library. YCISSatara Library is serving as a model for library computerization and electronic information services.

REFERENCES

1. Veenapani, S., Singh, I. &Others, (2009),Innovative practices in library services: A case study of Manipur University Library, 5th Convention PLANNER, Gauhati University, Guwahati, Pages 154-159.
2. Segal, J., Tyson, J. (1985), The Libraries Changing Role in Higher Education, Library Journal, Pages.44-46.
3. Shaheen, M., Christopher, K. (2009), Environment Intelligence: An Innovative Information Service, Singapore Journal of Library & Information Management, Volume 38, P. 13-26.

2

Best Practices of PCACS Learning Resource Centre, New Panvel

Sanjay B. Munavalli
Librarian, Pillai College of Arts,
Commerce & Science New Panvel-410206

ABSTRACT

This paper highlights the profile of the institution and learning resource centre of Pillai college of Arts,Commerce and Science,New Panvel.It also explains in detail the best practices followed by PCACS Learning Resource Centre (LRC) to promote it's knowledge resources and services .It also briefly describes how to identify and promote best practices in any type library .

Keywords : Pillai College, Best Practice, LRC, OSS, User

1. INTRODUCTION

Libraries and Information Centers are powerhouse of academic research and industrial setups. Information being a vital resource, PCACS Learning Resource Center would become an electron and just like an electron in orbit, it will work ceaselessly for its users. The library is the fulcrum of support for the entire range of activities in our campus.

The Learning Resource Center continues to be an essential component of the institute with outstanding vision and mission. The interest exhibited by Library Committee, Commitment of talented staff and the support of our management made the Library a most lively place on the campus providing a safe, comfortable and friendly environment that enable learning and advancement of knowledge promotes discovery and facilitates scholarship.

2. PROFILE OF PILLAI COLLEGE

Pillai College of Arts, Commerce and Science,Re-accredited “A” Grade by NAAC was established in 1998 by Dr. K. M. Vasudevan Pillai whose vision was to provide students of Navi Mumbai with quality education in a high-tech atmosphere. It is situated in a 10 acre land surrounded by natural beauty and supported by the best infrastructure facilities, a state-of-the-art conference room, well-equipped computer labs and well-stocked libraries.

3. PROFILE OF LEARNING RESOURCE CENTRE (LRC): "READ TO LEAD"

The Library has the collection of more than 24000 books, bound volumes of periodicals, In this collection there are good number of reference sources and noteworthy among them are vast number of Dictionaries, Encyclopedia of Britannica and almost all academic subjects.Apart from the above mentioned collection library has good number of collection on competitive exams, which forms a base for the students aspiring for such as Civil Services (UPSC), GMAT, CATetc.

Apart from regular collection an attractive feature is the amalgamation of Journals and Magazines, of which 8 Newspapers, 70 periodicals, which includes both subject as well as general. It is worth mentioning that approximate 2000 books are added to the Library every year. Apart from regular print collection LRC had good number of management CDs and Project Report CDs. It has established contacts with other organizations for exchange of the institution publications and inter-library loan arrangement.The collection is heavily used not only by our own students and faculty but by other sister institute students in our campus and others who walk in to use our library in large numbers.

3.1. Mission

"User satisfaction through Timely and Quality Service".

3.2. Vision

To serve as a catalyst for the development of an institution and its related activities and to actively participate in the fructification of the institution's plan of action.

3.3. Goals

- To give timely and quality information services to our users.

- To assist the users in upgrading their knowledge / skills in making proper use of library resources and services.
- To plan and design use of print and e-resources.
- To enable faculty members, students and other users of the library to become better informed in their field of specialization.
- To promote information literacy and e-learning.

3.4. Objectives

- To select, acquire, preserve and disseminate relevant and latest information to our users.
- To supply the latest information to all researchers in their respective fields in time.
- To procure the books and other reading materials requisitioned by faculty and students.
- To display news paper clippings and employment information on notice board.
- To provide computer based information services to all the users (Availability of books and other reading materials).

4. Best Practice : Meaning And Definitions

Best practices is a term dating back to the 1980s that was popularized by business writers,most notably Tom Peters and Robert Waterman in their bestseller *In Search of Excellence: Lessons from America's Best Run Companies (1982)*. Essentially, the term implies success; that certain actions,attitudes, and programs are the most efficient and effective way of doing business and that the same measures can be used with successful outcomes in all similar organizations.Adopting best practices can help enhance public relations and optimum utilization of knowledge resources of every type of library.

Best practices are defined by Jan Duffy as "processes that represent the most effective way of achieving a specific objective" (Skyrme, 2001)

"A practice qualifies to a Best practice status if it resulted in high value impact on any aspect of educational activity in an institution".

"Best practices are those that can be applied universally in public relations with assurance that such approaches will yield the most effective,responsible, and ethical performance and results."—*Encyclopedia of Public Relations, edited by Robert Heath*

According to ODLIS (Online Dictionary of Library and Information Science) best practices described as follows:"In the application of theory to real-life situations,procedures that, when properly, applied consistently yield superior results and are therefore used as reference points in evaluation of the effectiveness of alternative methods of accomplishing the same task. Best practices are identified by examining empirical evidence of success".

According to Oxford Advanced Learners Dictionary "best practices as quality of high standard, excellence, highly improved, outstanding, par excellence service. It means way of doing something that is usual or expected way in a particular organization or situation,guidelines for good practices. In this process of developing best practices we take action rather than good ideas, and we improve our skills."

"A set of guidelines, ethics or ideas that represent the most efficient or prudent course of action. Best practices are often set forth by an authority, such as a governing body or management, depending on the circumstances. While best practices generally dictate the recommended course of action, some situations require that such practices be followed."

5. BEST PRACTICES OF PCACS LEARNING RESOURCE CENTRE

5.1. Library Committee

The LRC has formed library committee to formulate policies and guidelines for the smooth functioning of library activities including student representatives from each branch.It helps students to participate in library related activities and to promote usage of learning resources.

5.2. Library Help Desk

The LRC has developed Library Help Desk where all library related documents like library information brochure,library membership form,demand slip,opinion book,feedback form,book requisition forms,inter library loan form,suggestion forms are made available to save the time of staff and library users.

5.3. Library Automation

The LRC has automated it's all activities through Koha-Open ILMS(Integrated Library Management Software) and bar-coded all knowledge resources.

5.4. Promotion of Open Source Software(OSS)

The PCAC LRC has adopted OSS like Kingsoft,Open Office for its' routine works.It has automated it's library activities through Koha-Open Integrated Library Management System and Dspace for archiving institution publications.

5.5. Digital Library

The library has developed Dspace-Digital Library to archive it's in house publications like question papers, lecture notes, project reports, staff publications, selected project reports and thesis of staff members new bulletin and syllabus.

5.6. Library Security

The library has installed CCTVs(Closed Circuit Televisions) to monitor student activities and fire extinguisher to prevent natural hazards.

5.7. Library Inter-Connectivity

The PCACS LRC has inter-connectivity with all Mahatma Education Society's institutions to share knowledge resources and information to meet the requirement of users in time.

5.7. Best Library User Awards

To promote and cultivate good reading habits among students and staff library has instituted best user award.The awards where distributed in college annual function.

5.8. Department Library

The library has is also assisting for the development and smooth functioning of departmental libraries by guiding the in-charge staff.

5.9. Information Literacy Program

The library is offering information literacy instruction program for freshers through print and non-print materials.The practical sessions regarding how to access N-LIST database ,Web-OPAC,Digital Library are conducting in Computer Labs.

5.10. Social Responsibility

The college as a social asset,it is our extended responsibility to outreach the general public so we are extending our library services to general public along with enrolled students and staff of our college.Our college library is started giving services to general public and alumni members by charging nominal charges.Under this scheme alumni members and the general public can become the members of our college library and get access to library.The members can refer our reference books,journals and magazines etc.and they can lend the library books,and photocopying services is also provided to them.

5.11. Arrangement of Resources

The LRC has classified it's knowledge resources according to globally recognized Dewey Decimal Classification System and arranged branch wise textbooks and reference books with barcode labels .Electronic resources arranged separately.

5.12. New Arrivals Display

Newly procured books displaying on New Arrival Display rack and same scanned cover pages posting through library e-mail group message to staff.Every month list of new books purchased are displayed branch wise on library notice board..It creates awareness among the students on the latest books available in their subject and also will help them in selection of books for their projects and assignments.

5.13. Book Exhibition

Annual book exhibition is organizing in which students and staff can recommend their desired book for library collection.The exhibition is open to all Mahatma Education Society's institution students and staff.The wide publicity is given through pamphlets and banners.

5.14. News Paper Clippings & Career Oriented Information

Important articles related to education, science, national and international persons, society concerned subjects and various scholarships and career oriented information is displaying on notice board and the same soft copies are circulated through online e-mail group message.It helps to know students know about various competitive opportunities and scholarships available in their selected field.

5.15. Library Membership

The library has a membership of TATA Institute of Social Sciences,British Council My Library,DELNET to meet the research requirement of our users.

5.16. Thought for the Day

Displaying daily basis for students in front of library display board to provoke intellectual discussion.

5.17. Special Care for Differently abled persons

Library is situated on ground floor with good natural ventilation and it easy to enter through wheel chair.Personal assistance from library staff also providing.

5.18. Open Access System

To save the time of user and staff and to get access to their desired knowledge resource PCACS LRC follows open access system.

5.19. Library Publicity

The library has separate website to display about its collection, staff, arrangement, rules and services available for students.It has provided links to important websites, Web-OPAC and N-LIST and other databases subscribed by institution. Apart from this library information also made available through library information update brochure, college prospectus, college magazine, news bulletin, also publishing annual report.

5.20. Stock Verification & Weed out of Books

The PCACS LRC is annually conducting stock verification to measure it's strengths and weaknesses and to take necessary actions. It also periodically weeding old syllabus books, magazines and newspapers to save space and time of users.

5.21. Special Provision for Economically and Socially Backward Students

Such category students offered extra books lending for more than normal lending period without any dues.

5.22. Library Use Statistics

Data is captured through registers maintained at all service points and circulation statistics where captured from Koha made available monthly on notice board to create healthy competitiveness among students branch wise and make optimum utilization of resources.

5.23. Students Participation

The students who enrolled for University of Mumbai, Department of Lifelong Learning & Extension activity are allowed to work in library. It imparts knowledge about the library and development of a positive outlook and attitude in students and awareness about the value of a library and its services. In addition, the maintenance staff is benefited by the assistance of students. Apart from this library is enrolling interns from other institution also to learn library management and development techniques.

5.24. Patron Driven Acquisition

Specialty of Patron Driven Acquisition (PDA) is that it enables the users in selecting and acquiring reading materials. Such reading material is highly used and appreciated reading material. The current trend in acquisition of reading material indicates that libraries are trying to acquire reading materials with patron's initiatives.

5.25. Provision of E-books and E-journals

The library has a membership of UGC N-LIST through which our users can access more than 2,500 e-journals and 1,10,607 e-books. Apart form this British Council Library, DOAJ, DOAB facilities are also provided.

6. HOW TO IDENTIFY AND PROMOTE BEST PRACTICES:

The essence of identifying best practices is "transferring knowledge from those who know how to do something well to those who are keen to learn more" (Skyrrne, 2001).There are four best practices used by libraries of all sizes and types to help enhance our image and promote the many services we provide to our patrons. The following are top four choices for identifying and promoting best practices in libraries according to Adeen Poster (2006)

6.1. Know Your Patrons and Give Them What They Want

To know your audience,ask your patrons what they most want from your library and be willing to meet that need.

6.2. The Customer is Always Right

It really means that we should trust our customers and believe that their opinions, desires, and experiences are valid..Checking our hiring and training processes to make sure the people we have at service points are capable and trained to really listen to our users and their problems. There are lots of customer service classes, articles, and books for staff that will reinforce the service ethic and make it a conscious part of the transaction between us, or our staff member, and the patron.No matter what size library we work in,if our staff can't help a user, find someone or something that can. Even a simple referral to another library or another library colleague can help the user find whatever it is he or she needs. Yes, we all provide inter iibrary loan service and reference assistance, but just the fact that these services are available in a library doesn't mean they are visible, so be sure all our users know about them through good promotion and publicity.

6.3. Be Creative, Try Something New, Be Proactive

Reaching out to our patrons will pay off dramatically in their positive attitudes toward us and the services and resources we offer. Start an electronic newsletter,online group or targeting a population of our users that we think might gain help by the library, which can be accomplished by something as simple as a personal visit to an office.

6.4. Recognize and Reward Value—Especially if it's Your Own

Have you, your library, or a staff member won an award or accomplished something special? Let everyone in your organization know! Celebrating the award is more than just an excuse to throw a party—it is also an opportunity to market the intrinsic value of the library to your patrons. If they see that others value your work, they will too.The same recognition is warranted if you just completed a major research assignment for a partner or faculty member.Let everyone in your organization know what you can do, and they will ask you to provide a similar service for them in no time at all.No matter how small, or big, your organization is, you can use these maxims to create programs, initiatives, new policies,procedures, and customer service-focused staff training to best demonstrate your collections and services to your patrons.

CONCLUSION

A best practice is a practice which paves the way for enhancing an existing function and helps in effective implementation or use of the process. Use of technology in designing and delivering the information products and services in a library has always yielded good results. Automation of all in-house operations in academic libraries wit bar-coding, user identity and web-OPAC facilities is a best practice in totality of library services. Effective implementation of user education/ awareness programs with the new techniques and tools will also be a best practice in extent of use of library services.

Developing digital repositories with subject content, open sources and institutional information and customizing it to internal requirements with remote access is one of the globally adopted best practices in the university libraries. In the present era of IT, the academic libraries need to re-orient to the highly qualitative information collection and services.

REFERENCES

1. Retrieved from *http://www.investopedia.com/terms/b/best_practices.asp*
2. Postar A (2006),Use best practices to promote your library,AASL Spectrum,p.12-13
3. Skyrme, D.J. (2001), Are your best practices really the best?, Retrieved from *www.skyrme.com/ updates/u54_f1.htm*
4. Jolie O. Graybill Maria Taesil Hudson Carpenter Jerome Offord Jr Mary Piorun Gary Shaffer, (2013), "Employee on boarding : identification of best practices in ACRL libraries", Library Management,34(3)., pp.200-218 Retrieved from *http://dx.doi.org/10.1108/01435121311310897*
5. Davidson, M. (2008), Concerto for the Left Hand, University of Michigan Press, Ann Arbor, MI.
6. Baird, R.M., Rosenbaum, S.E. and Toombs, S.K. (2009), Disability: The Social, Political and Ethical Debate, Prometheus Books, Amherst, NY.
7. Sue Samson, (2011), "Best practices for serving students with disabilities", Reference Services Review, 39(2)., pp.260-277 Retrieved from http://dx.doi.org/10.1108/00907321111135484
8. Retrieved from www.pcacs.ac.in

3

Innovative Services in Sardar Vallabhabhai Patel Arts and Science College Ainpur (SVPCA) Library

Rahul B. Khandare
Librarian, S.V.P. Arts & Science College,
Ainpur, Tal. Raver, Dist. Jalgaon (M.S.)- 425507

Shashank S. Sonwane
Assistant Professor, Dept. of Library and
Information Science, Dr. Babasaheb Ambedkar
Marathwada University, Aurangabad (M.S.) – 431004

ABSTRACT

The present case study of SVPCA library has started many best practices and is in continuous process by following NAAC's set of best practices guideline in college libraries. They are very simple and easy to adopt. Value addition is brought out by the best practices.

Keywords : Innovative Services, Best Practice, SVPCA Library, NAAC, e-resources

1. INTRODUCTION

It is time to identify and adopt the new ways that will lead library and information Centre to improve their process and activities, thereby optimizing the resource utilization and delivering high quality, and value added services to their users. In the process of institutional accreditation, libraries have a crucial role. The services of the libraries have been expanding as they contribute significantly to the learning process, particularly the e-learning process. In the accreditation process, evaluation of libraries is an essential component, where the collection, services and their outreaching capacity are monitored. College libraries need to have facilities that promote effective and interactive access and use of information resources for all users. In the area of physical facilities, the libraries need to offer safe, comfortable, well-lighted, clean space, with adequate and appropriate seating arrangements to ensure effective use of the library's resources including digital resources. The libraries need to prepare well-framed rules and guidelines with regard to hours of access, circulation policies, and other regulations to offer better services to the users. Best practices are nothing but developing tailor made services, reaching beyond with available resources and delighting the customers.

2. MEANING AND DEFINITION OF BEST PRACTICE

Best practices are nothing but developing tailor made services, reaching beyond with available, resources and delighting the customers, quality of high standard, excellence, and highly improved, outstanding, par excellence service. It means way of doing something that is usual or expected way in a particular organization or situation, guidelines for good practices (Vaishnav, 2013).

According to National Board of Accreditation and Assessment (NAAC) "Best practice may be innovative and be a philosophy, policy, strategy, programme, process or practice that solved a problem or create new opportunities and positively impact on organizations".

3. WHY INNOVATIVE/BEST PRACTICES IN COLLEGE LIBRARIES?

- To execute the five laws of library science
- To magnetize and meet the user demand
- To maximize the utilization of the library
- To identify the need of the users
- To market library services and products

4. ABOUT SARDAR VALLABHABHAI PATEL ARTS & SCIENCE COLLEGE, AINPUR

To provide higher education for liable, needy, economically backward and specially for women's, the members of the Ainpur Parisar Shikshan Prasarak Mandal established Sardar Vallabhabhai Patel Arts & Science College in June 1993. The College is affiliated to the North Maharashtra University, Jalgaon and registered under 2(f) and 12(b) at UGC. College runs co-education. College has its own campus with essential well equipped building. The College is accredited by NAAC in 2004; now in reaccreditation under process. APSPM's hardly promoting higher education for rural masses since 20 years. College has utilized XIth Plan grant for women's hostel, sports center, general development and some carrier oriented programs. Institute being run by farmers, the basic element of financial source for our nation who continuously suffers from natural disasters, financial irregularities, water resources since past decades. Apart from this our management continuously encourages us for further development. The most proude achievement of College is Best College 2011-12, Awarded by North Maharashtra University, Jalgaon.

5. INNOVATIVE SERVICES FOLLOWED AT SVPCA LIBRARY

Electronic resources : SVPCA library subscribing N-List from last three years.

Fig. 1. N-List

Internet Centre : Information communication technologies growing very fast in all sectors, libraries are not exception for this. Therefore SVPCA library providing internet facility to the users. There are five computers for accessing internet.

Computerization : It is not possible to all academic libraries to become a digital library or electronic library. But today, the demand and needs of the library users are changing; they need services within moment/minutes. The automation of library is under process. SOUL 2.0 software has been purchased for library automation.

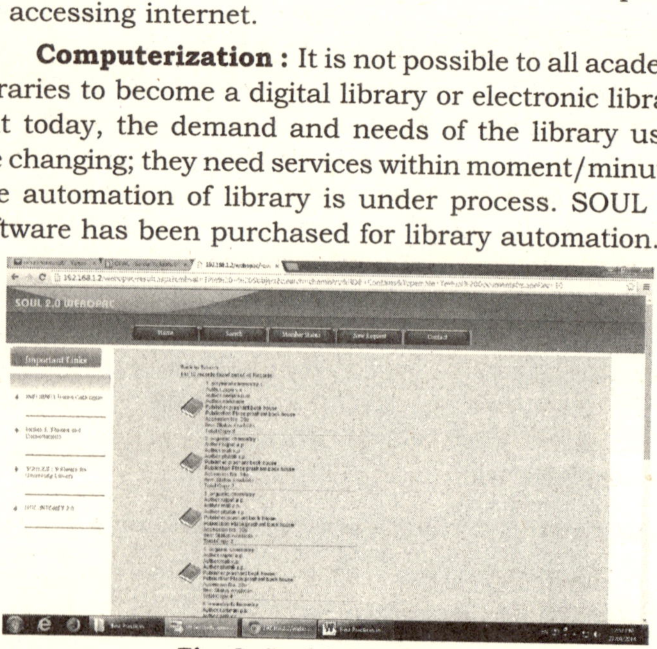

Fig. 2. Soul 2.0 Software

Inter Library Loan : There is an Agreement of Inter Library Loan with two nearby college libraries namely Shri. V.S. Naik College, Raver and D.N. College Faizpur.

Library Portal (www.sites.google.com/site/svpcalibrary) : SVPCA library has developed separate website to provide the information of library to the users including Library rules, services, open access resources/ N-List/OPAC links, Student Corner (competitive examination, university website link), important website links, provision of new arrivals books list etc.

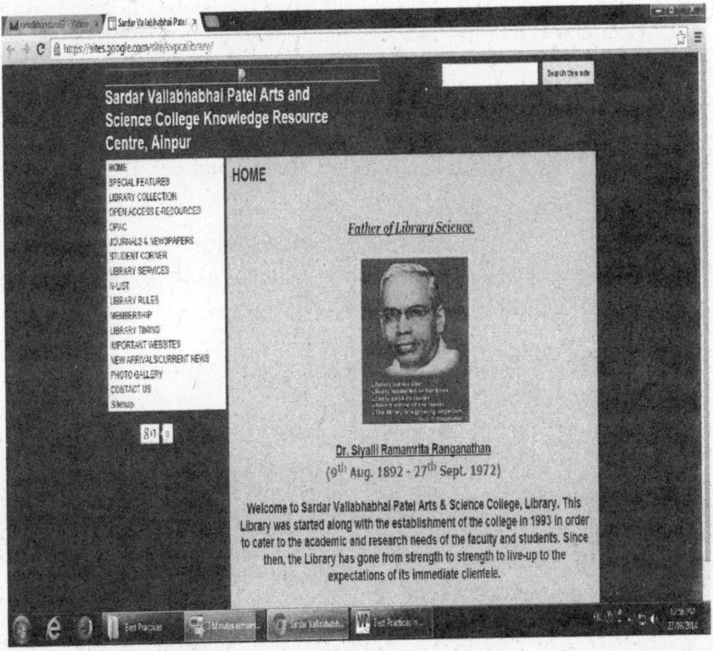

Fig. 3. Library Portal

Competitive Quiz : SVPCA Library is organizing Quiz for their users such as General Knowledge Examination at least one in a year. Library organizing this activity from last three years.

Fig. 4. Quiz Competition Prize Distribution

Book Exhibition : The main aim of book exhibition to know the library resources, collection to their users, SVPCA library organizing book exhibition at least one time in academic year since last three years.

Fig. 5. Book Exhibition

Suggestion Box : as students have to face many problems and difficulties there is suggestion box which is kept in library to write chits and their suggestions which are helpful to get user feedback and to improve library services.

Alerting services : SVPCA library providing e-mails service to the staff members including Seminar/ Conferences information, Articles, Newspaper Clipping, and University Circulars etc.

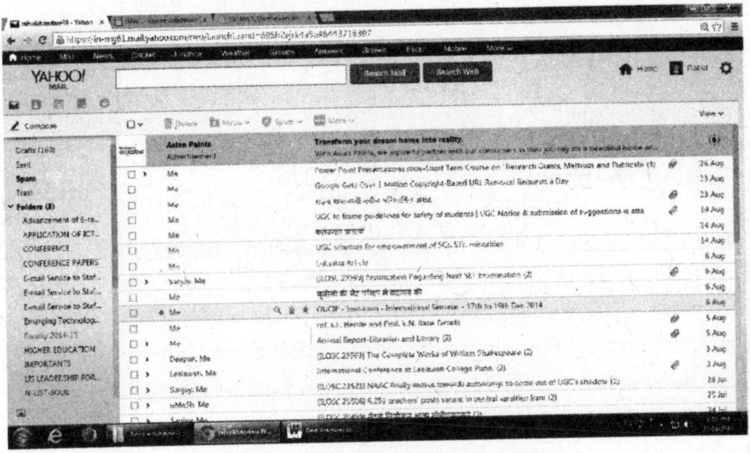

Fig. 6. E-mail alert service

Users Feedback : SVPCA library conducting library feedback forms from students from last academic year; and improving library services as per users demand.

Reprography/Print Service : Library provides Reprography/Print Service in nominal price. It's one way to attract the users to the library.

Book Bank Scheme : Library provides book bank facility to students in academic year.

Best Library User Award : SVPCA library sponsoring 'Dr. Babasaheb Ambedkar Best Library User Award' from last three year. Attendances in library, discipline, books circulation are the basic criteria for this award. Library advisory committee announce this award in annual gathering function.

Fig. 7. Best Library User Award Prize Distribution

Use of Facebook : Today social networking sites playing important role in society to share knowledge, ideas. Librarians can also use those social networking sites for user services, such as some news, recruitment, slogans, new arrivals in library etc.

Fig. 8. Library Facebook Page 'svpca'

Library Orientation : SVPCA library conducts library hour, library tour at the beginning and mid-term of the semester and guide to users regarding library and library facilities, services, its collection and how to access information available in the library and available etc.

Library Hour : SVPCA library organized library hour for new comers students in the start and end of the year.

Fig. 9. Library hour Programme

Career Opportunity Centre/Newspaper Clipping Point : There is a separate notice board for career opportunities advertisement, newspaper clipping, important articles etc.

6. PROBLEMS AND PROSPECTS IN APPLYING BEST PRACTICES IN SVPCA LIBRARY

- Limited staff in library
- Lack of Time
- Rural Area
- Problem of failure electricity
- illiterate users regarding Latest technologies and concepts in handling of information
- Students are not interesting to access e-resources through N-List.

- Students are not ready to borrow books from ILL Library.
- 80% students don't have their e-mail Id.

7. CONCLUSION

Use of technology in designing and delivering the information products and services has always made good results. Hence adopting new techniques and tools in imparting user education may be of best practice inn extent of use of library services. The best practices adopted should bridge the gap between the library and the users for effective and maximum utilization of the resources, which will result in the advancement and promotion of higher educational goals and the vision and mission of the library. Many library stakeholders grumble that any best practice means involvement of a lot of resources especially in terms of money and equipment's. In fact it requires active participation, willingness, creativity and problem solving attitude from the library stakeholders. Developing best practices, analyzing and revising them at a regular interval will lead to continuous improvement in overall performance of the library and the whole institution.

REFERENCES

- Chandran, D. & Kumar, Kutty (2013). Best practices in the management of academic libraries: A few recommendations of NAAC. In Nilima R. Bankar (Ed.), *Innovations and Best practices in Library Administration*. Proceedings of UGC sponsored National Conference (pp. 35-36). Aurangabad, India.
- Dhamdhere, Sangeeta N. (2012). Changing Face of Academic Libraries. PEARL - A Journal of Library and Information Science, 6(1), 8-13.
- http://ainpurcollege.org/02_About/Default.aspx
- http://naac.gov.in/docs/Guidelines-Colleges-Library.pdf
- Khandare, R.B., Mukhyadal, B.G. & Khandare, S.B. (2014). Best Practices In College Library-Special Reference to Sardar

Vallabhabhai Patel Arts And Science College Library. In Rameshwar Pawar (Ed.), *Best Practices In The College Libraries.* Proceedings of UGC sponsored National Conference (pp. 23-24). Purna, Dist. Parbhani, Maharashtra, India.

- Pragasam, P. Arul (2013). Article Indexing Initiative: A Novel Best Practice. In Nilima R. Bankar (Ed.), *Innovations and Best practices in Library Administration.* Proceedings of UGC sponsored National Conference (pp. 237-238). Aurangabad, India.
- Prasad, V.S. (n.d.). Guidelines on Quality Indicators in Library and Information Services: Affiliated/Constituent Colleges. Available at http://naac.gov.in/docs/Library-Guidelines-Universities.pdf accessed on 13 Jan. 2015.
- Tikam, Madhuri V. (2010). Best Practices in Academic Libraries. Available at http://liscompendium.wordpress.com/article/bestpracticesinacademiclibraries35muq6i9t1aro3/ accessed on 19 Dec. 201.4
- Umesh, K. Y. (2012). Best practices adopted in academic libraries and information resource centers. *International Journal of Information Dissemination and Technology,* 2(3), 186-188.
- Vaishnav, A.A. (2013). Innovations and Best practices in Library Administration. In Nilima R. Bankar (Ed.), *Innovations and Best practices in Library Administration.* Proceedings of UGC sponsored National Conference (pp. 13-27). Aurangabad, India.

4

Best Practices of Chetana's H. S. College of Commerce & Economics and Smt. Kusumati Chaudhri College of Art, Bandra

Sanjay Narayan More
Chetana's H.S. College of Commerce & Economics
Kusumati Chaudhri
College of Art, Bandra (E) Mumbai 400051.

ABSTRACT

This article examines the various aspects involved in creation of a Library web portal. It highlights the importance of prior planning of this process. The process of registration of domain name for web portal, the various options and technologies involved in the hosting and uploading of a website are explained using the case of Chetana library portal.

Keywords: Library portal, Library services, Web portal, OPAC

1. INTRODUCTION

Web Portals are hotter than hot and newer than tomorrow, Believe it or not, no organization that aspires beyond the neighborhood grocery store level will be able to survive out in the new century without a web portal/ website. The computer age has brought in the facility of fast access to information. A library portal serves as an integrated interface to a wide variety of digital resources and web based library services. Web portals are also important tools for users to access and utilize library and information services over a network. An informative home page provides the users helpful information about the library, its collection and services. In addition, library portal also host the link to important internet resources useful for the library.

2. BEST PRACTICE OF YOUR COLLEGE LIBRARY: LIBRARY PORTAL

A portal is a single user interface for accessing wide variety of electronic resources, both within and outside the library. The portal technology has enabled librarians to shift to a more proactive, user- centered and service oriented model of library. The web page of a library is not only an excellent medium for publishing the library activities but also mechanism for accessing its resources and services.

Library portal is the website, which helps to get information by providing access to all relevant e-resources at one point.

Planning for the Web Portal

For designing, good planning is the basic step to be considered. One should have an idea of how he wants to design the page. Some of the important points to be considered while designing a home page are as:

Objectives

1. Home page is content page and should provide links to all the necessary pages.
2. Should provide links to the principal or higher level home pages.

Responsibility

1. Responsible person has to look into the contents that go in www collections.
2. Right decision should be taken regarding the documents which may go public.
3. Care should be taken while transferring the information. An error at this point could produce problems at the final stage.
4. Electronic version should get released before the published version.

Accuracy and timeliness of the information

1. Ensure accuracy regarding the information for public use.
2. Contents in the web portal should not have missing links.
3. Spelling and syntax should be proper.
4. Links should be verified.
5. Consistency in the style is to be followed on all the pages.

Forming Web Portal Development Team

The website development and maintenance team play an important role in creating the web portal. You should form a website development group with the library staff with technical knowledge about the computer technology, which will include following professionals:

1. Designer : Designing the new pages or change the design of existing pages.

2. Content Provider : The person should be responsible for developing and providing the contents which will be uploaded on the web portal.

3. Proof Reader : Checking up the matter put up on the site for any mistakes.

4. Photographer : To provide the pictures of various events, happenings etc.

5. Co-coordinator : Co-ordinate with various departments to keep the contents of the website updated.

6. Public Relation Officer : To interact with general users and convey to the technical team the various changes required for the better interaction between the website and the users.

Registering Your Domain Name

The first thing to do is to get an address for the website in cyberspace. This is called the domain name registration, for example *www.chetanalibrary.webs.com.* There are two broad types of domain names 1. Generic top level domains of .org, .net, .mil, and 2. Country specific domain names like .in for India and .sg for Singapore.

Advantages of Web-Portal

- Library user need not to go to the library physically.
- User can get access the information at any time.
- The same resources can be used at the same time by a number of users.
- Library Portal provides very user friendly interfaces, giving clickable access to its resources.
- The cost of maintaining a library portal is very less.

Welcome to the Chetana Library Portal

Chetana Library developed its Library Portal with the help of free website provider. To set up a site, one will need space on a web server to store all HTML documents. There are many sites on the Internet that give free web space. Here we made free portal with **www.webs.com** a commercial cum free service provider, who help us to create own web portal. Follow the following easy steps to make your own library portal:

1. Sign-in on webs.com with the help of your email id.
2. Next you will be asked to fill in a few details, like your domain address, description of your page, a topic that best describes your page etc.
3. Select professional design of theme for your web portal.
4. Add dynamic pages like About Library, Services, e-data base, and Contact etc.
5. Include powerful apps like Web Store, blog or Hyper link etc.
6. Add your content: Brand your site header with your library logo.
7. Drag and drop content areas like slideshow, forms and maps.
8. Publish and Share: Launch your website with a single click.

CHETAHA LIBRARY PORTAL DIAGRAM

HOME ABOUT SERVICES E-DATABASE RULS JOURNALS NOTICE ALBUMS CONTACT

1. HOME PAGE : This is a content page and should provide links to all the necessary pages. So, we give our college founder's inspirational speech, some important library photography slide show and one hyper link of library Web Catalogue.

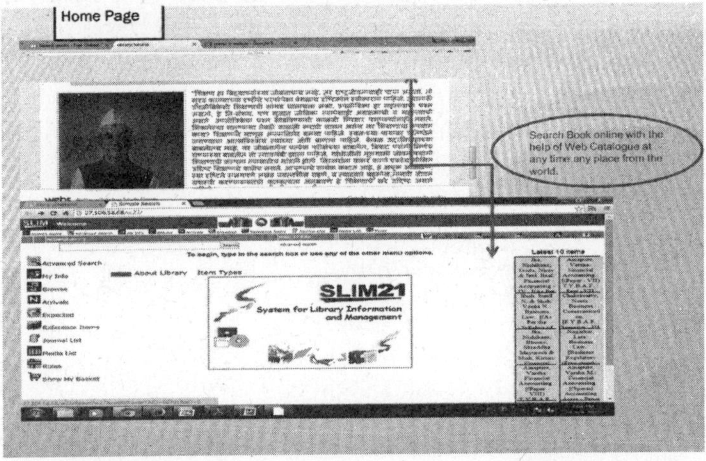

2. ABOUT : Here we give whole information about library like Collection, Function, Department, Timing and objectives of the library.

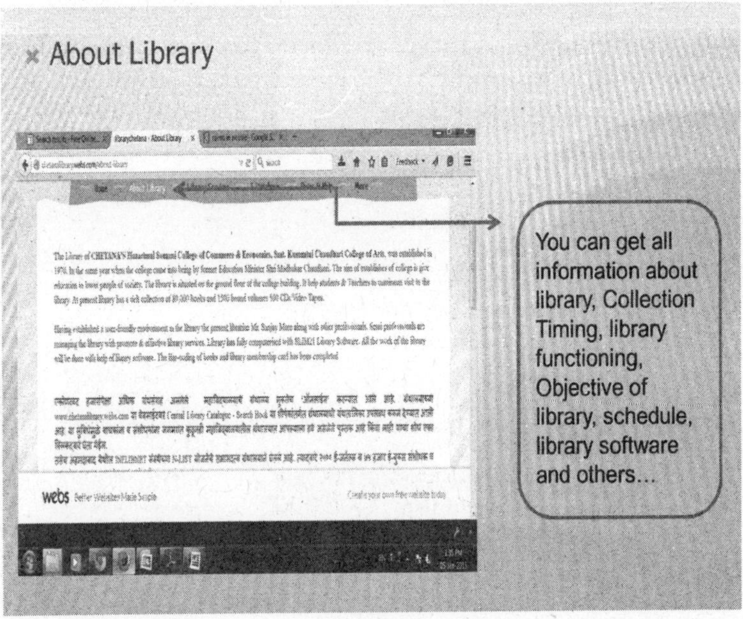

3. SERVICES : Here we give information of library services, activities like User Orientation, Book Exhibition, Best library user award etc.

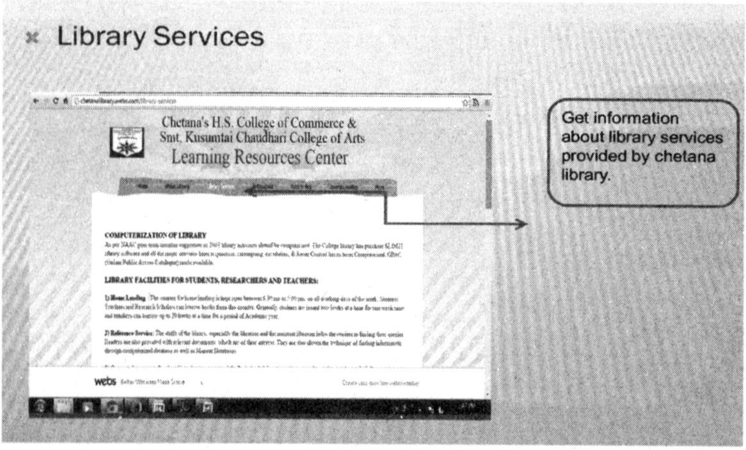

4. E-DATABASE : Here we uploaded Syllabus; Question Papers with the help of Google Drive which is easily retrievable and downloadable from anywhere and anytime on internet. We have also given link of ugc inflibnet n-list e-database link that provides us 25000 e-journals and75000 E-books online, which are accessible anytime. We also have given some important links, which help the students in their academic study.

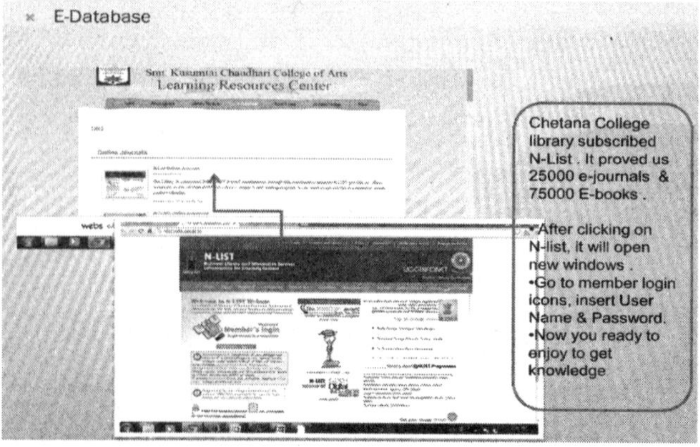

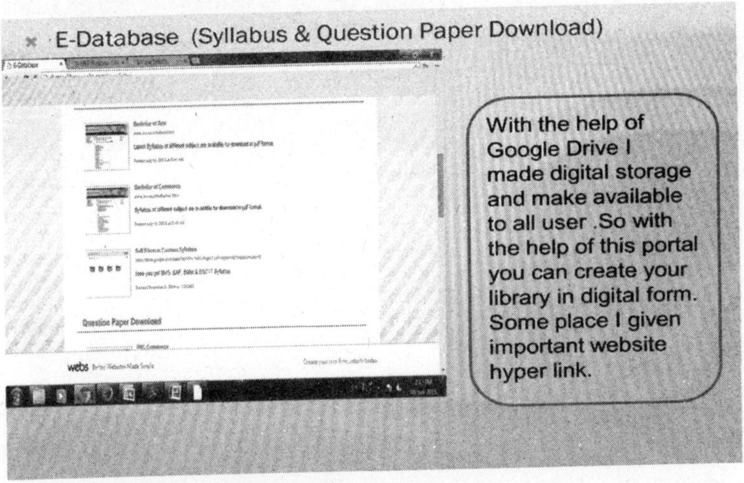

5. RULE AND HELP : Most of the library members don't know library basic rules, what types of service are there and how to get book, service, online database etc. In this menu we have given basic library rules and one guideline chart given which help user to get familiar with library.

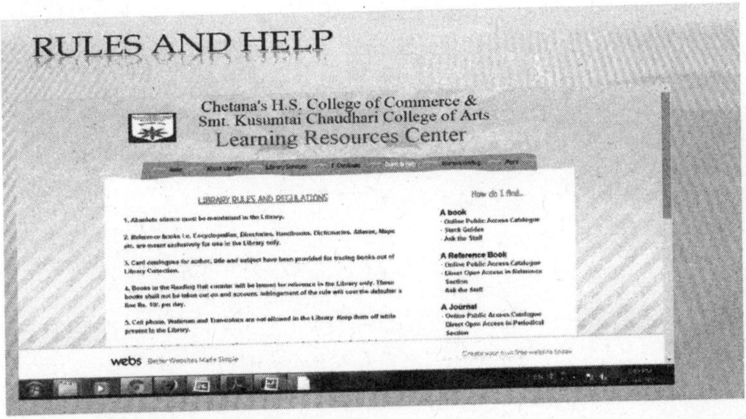

Online Suggestion Box : Here Users can suggest their ideas, opinions, and rise query about library with the help of online suggestion box. These suggestions directly go to the librarian's email account, enabling the librarian to act on query by checking the mail daily.

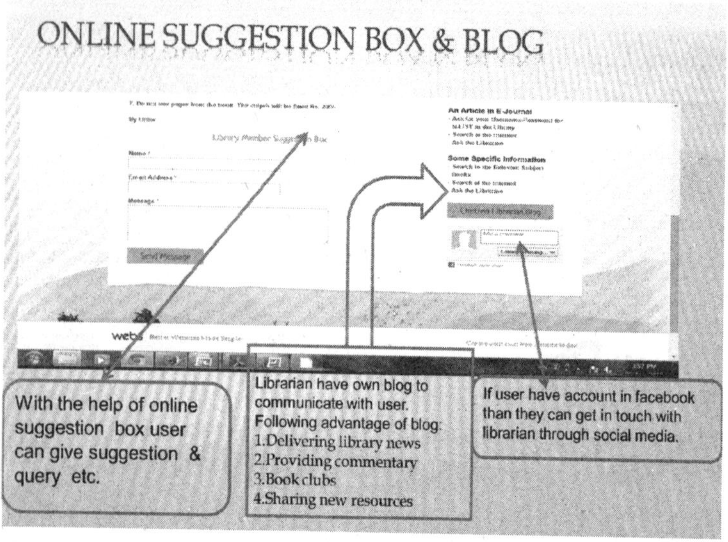

6. JOURNALS HOLDING : Here you get the list of Magazines/Journals available in the library and also get information about number of Newspapers and back volumes available.

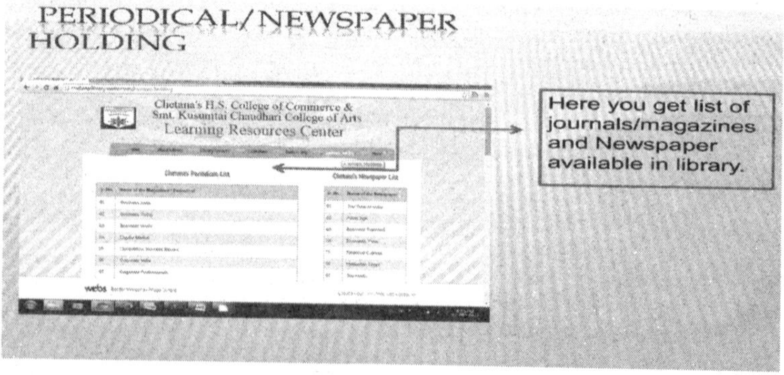

7. LIBRARY NOTICE : It is a very important menu for users and staff. Here we give all library notices online, so that the users get updated information.

LIBRARY NOTICE

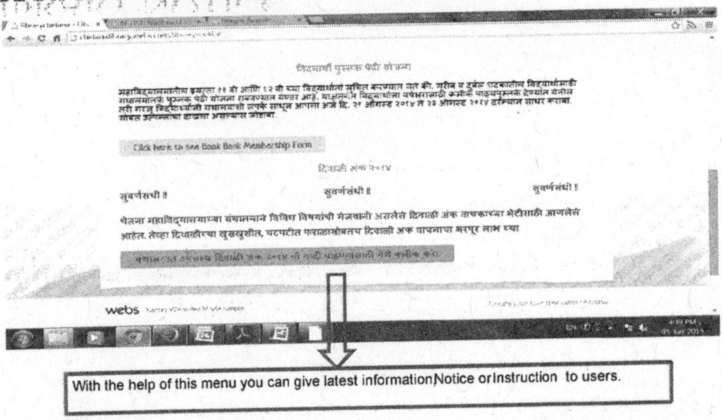

8. PHOTO GALLERY : In this menu we store photographs of functions arranged by the college library and make them available to users.

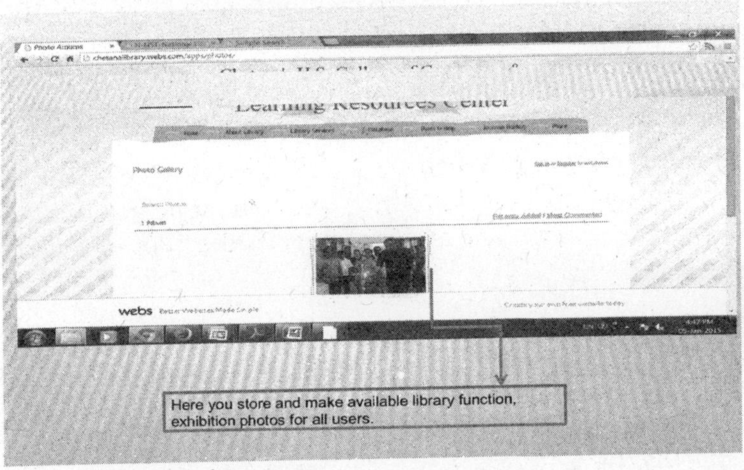

9. CONTACT US : Here we gave contact information of librarian and Google supportive area map, which help us to reach Chetana Library.

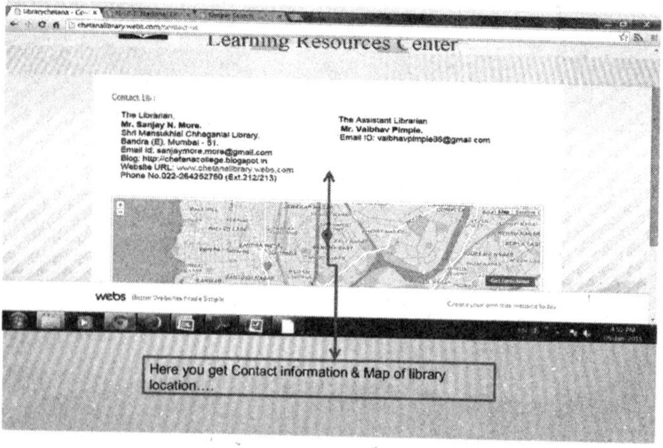

5. CONCLUSION

With the rapid advancement in computer technology along with information technology, libraries and information centers have been blessed with electronic materials and therefore libraries are gradually shifting towards the electronic libraries with electronic resources therefore libraries are increasingly involved in creating and acquiring e-resources such as Library Portal, Website, Digital library etc. The Library portal is very useful for the information provider and it is also very effective in the college library. Students and teachers get library information very fast and easily with the help of smart phone.

REFERENCES

1. Aadhavan, Omesh (2010). Development of Digital Library. Oxford Book Company: Delhi. Page No. 10-27.
2. Tripathi, Raghuvendra(Ed.) & Raj, Hans (Ed.)(2012). Emerging Technologies in Managing Library and Information Services. DPS Publication: New Delhi. Page No.31-86.
3. OCLC (2003). Libraries and the enhancement of e-learning. Ohio: Online Computer Library Center Inc.
4. Pandey, S.K.(2007). Encyclopedia of Library Automation Systems and Networking Series, Almond Publication: New Delhi. Page No. 25-45.
5. *http://www.webs.com*

5

Best Practices in Library of R.N.C. Arts, J.D.B. Commerce And N.S.C. Science College, Nashik Road

Ravindra B. Bagul

Librarian, R.N.C. Arts, J.D.B.Commerce & N.S.C. Science College, Nashik Road

ABSTRACT

In this research paper, the focus is on the effective use of ICT & the best practices to provide better liberary facilities to the reader fraternity in our college.

Keywords : Academic Libraries, Library, Services, Best Practices.

INTRODUCTION

The Government of India aappointed a University Commission to look into the condiditon of universities and make recommendations to improve them. The University Education Commission of 1948, under the chairmanship of Dr. S. Radhakrishnan, saw the poor conditions of academic libraries also and suggested that better facilities, budgets, grants, references, and bibliorgaphic services be provided in all academic libraries. However, it was only after the establishment of the University Grants Commission in 1953 that some attention was given to the academic libraries of India. A survey done in 1957, revealed that the libraries were still ill-equipped, inadequate, and "the plight of libraries was for from happy". On the recommendation of the UGS's Library Committee of 1957, chaired by Dr. S.R. Ranganathan, a few much-needed improvements were made for the benefit of the students, faculty, and other users. The Kothari Commission of 1964-66, surveyed the higher education system of the country and looked into the condition of academic libraries also.

BEST PRACTICES

Definition : Oxford English Dictionary describes 'Best Practices as quality of most excellent or desireable type or most appropriate, advantageous, highly improved, outstanding, par excellence services or the customary or expected procedure or way of doing something that is usual or expected way in a particular organization or situation, guidelines for good practices. In this process of developing best practices we take action rather than good ideas, and we improve our skills.

ODLIS (Online Dictionary of Library and Information Science) describes best practices as follows :

"In the application of theory to real-life situations, procedures that, when properly applied, consistently yield superior results and are therefore used as reference points in evaluating the effectiveness of alternative methods of accomplishing the same task. Best Practices are identified by examining empirical evidence of success

R.N.C. Arts, J.D.B.Commerce & N.S.C. Science College, Nashik Road : A Study

PURPOSE AND OBJECTIVES

R.N.C. Arts, J.D.B.Commerce & N.S.C. Science College, Nashik Road. LATE BALRAM HEMRAJ LAHOTI

Library was Established in the year 1963 to support the academic and extra-curricular objectives of the college.

THE OBJECTIVES OF THE LIBRARY ARE

1. To participate effectively in the college programme as it strives to meet the reading and information needs to students, teachers and ex. Readers.
2. Provide services and reading material to the student so as to enable them to use the library for referring to textbooks reference books and pursue independent study.
3. Provide services and reading material to the teaching faculty of the college so as to enable them to use library for preparing lecturer, counting education and research.
4. Provide orientation user education and references service to the teachers and students in order to maximize the use of the library.
5. To support the extra-curricular activities conducted by the college.

INTRODUCTION

R.N.C. Arts, J.D.B.Commerce & N.S.C. Science College, Nashik Road was established in 1963 with a view to provide education to the student community in Nashik Road and its vicinity.

To support this matter of the college, Library was started during the same year with a small collection of books and started to support various programmers of the college. Now the Library has collection of (95658) books on various subjects and there for plays in important role in this direction. The library is centrally located in the campus which located the area of 7000 sq. fit. construction. The library is well ventilated with adequate facilities.

The college regularly subscribes about 139

Journals, Magazine and Periodicals. There is Ten Computers and purchased Library Software which is used for all Library work.

The library is attached with a Reading Hall with the seating capacity of around 100 students. The library also provides a separate reference section along with independent seating arrangement. The library also provides separate internet facility it help the students, teacher.

The library is open from 7.30 am to 5.00 pm on all working days including vacations.

BEST PRACTICES IN ACADEMIC LIBRARIES

Library Advisory Committee : It comprises of the following Principal as the Chairman, Librarian the Secretary and one member each from Arts, Science and Commerce faculty, one member of accountant and one representative elected student.

Orientation programme : The fresh students at the beginning of each academic year the importance of the library, thereby exposing the students to its various sections of the library, the library resources and the various library services.

Book Bank Facility : Is available since the last 15 years is our college for SC, ST student under these scheme students are provided the set of books required for their study each academic year.

Library Book Exhibition : Our College Library is arrange the book exhibition to various publishers and distributors. The student see the latest books and the aware of the books.

Users Feedback : Our College library feedback form to teachers and students and ask them to note their response and filling the details providing better service to the teachers and student fraternity.

OPAC : Our library provides the OPAC facility to

the Teachers and Students. They came on the library and the search the books on OPAC.

Web Based Services : The library can provide various web service through our library such as, full text article, e-book, e-journal (Through the link of N-List programme), Thesis and dissertation.

CONCLUSION

To sum up, these paper studies & notes observations on the objective on the library, collection of books & cds, the role of management & administration in enhancing library facility & create awareness among the students in our college.

REFERENCES

1. Sharma N. R., (1986), Indian Academic Libraries and S.R. Ranganathan : A Critical Study, Sterling Publishing, Banglore.
2. Concise Oxford English Dictionary, (2007) Catherine Soanes & Angus Stevension (edit).2nd New Delhi, Oxford University Press.
3. Reitz, Joan M. Online Dictionary for Library and Information Services :(Online) available from : *http://www.abc-clio.com/ODLIS/seachODLIS.aspd* (Accessed on dt. 14.03.2012
4. Vyas, S.D. (2009) Best Practices in Academic Libraries in India : A study, In : Proceeding of International Conference on Academic Library. 2009, 5th 8th Oct. India, New Delhi, Delhi University Library System, University of Delhi.

6

Best Practices in Academic College Libraries With Reference to BMCC Library

Damodar Dasharath Waghmare
Librarian, Willingdon College, Sangli

ABSTRACT

This is the modern era of advances in almost all fields of human growth. Emerging information explosion and the revolution in science - technology and communication are affecting day to day transactions and interactions all over the world. Worldwide social, economical, political, educational, industrial and cultural organizations are proving as backbone of the sole existence and development of human being. Libraries and information centers are playing an important role in keeping well informed these organizations and the society as whole, with most up-to-date information. Therefore services provided by such information centers are very significant. Also in this IT era, the role of the libraries and information centers has been changed drastically. They have to deal with all types of novel technology. They have to be familiar with the new and universal trends in handling the information and providing prompt as well as accurate services. In field of higher education, the Academic Libraries have vital role to play. Library of Brihan Maharashtra College of Commerce, Pun is a leading commerce library In Maharashtra, shouldering its responsibility towards catering the information requirements of upcoming leadership in the field of commerce, trade, banking and economics. In our paper, taking BMCC library as a case study, an attempt has been made to highlight the best practices adopted in the mode of delivering the library services.

Keywords : Academic College Library, Commerce Library, BMCC Library ICT Environment, Best Practices

1. INTRODUCTION

Lord Buddha enlightened that everything related to human behavior should change or restructure along with the global standards to solve the human problems. The Good deeds are acquiring every person, organization, country to establish human welfare. Every man, society and nation must have universal standards to do the best practices for creation of ideal work for ideal behavior for all people on the Earth.

Libraries are the social institution which is responsible and committed the management of collection, dissemination of right information at right time in right way to the right readers. Doing best practices are higher standard of any library for their reader's welfare. Wide attitude and future needs to cater the services for clientele, society and country development. The World development revolves around the economic and trade affairs due to globalization. Every activity got changed and close to each other because of globalization. Every LIS professional should have love about human, other animal and nature. They must have love with knowledge, morality and wisdom to discharge best practices. Librarian should committed with profession and do best practices for our young generation which is responsible to establish new nation. Librarian should have a great man to think globally and act globally. He must possess high social standard in front of young clientele in higher education process. Academic library play a great role in higher education system in India. In India, the growth rate of higher education is very low in comparison with the other countries in the world because of social imbalance. Therefore infront of academic library there are more challenges to increase standard of higher standard of higher education system. To face these challenges library and LIS professional should practice best practices in their library and discharge better services for lifelong learning.

1.1. Academic Library

Academic library is defined as "Academic library is a library that is attached to the higher education institutions which serves two complementary purposes, to support the curriculum of the institute and to support the research of the university faculty and students". Academic libraries are playing a very essential and fundamental role in higher education. It acquires, processes, organizes, the basic information sources and disseminate the vital information to students, faculties and the research scholars for the growth of the higher education. Ultimately it supports the research work going on in various branches of knowledge all over the nation. Information explosion and the emerging information and technology has changed the higher education development worldwide. Therefore the academic libraries are also on the verge of changing its conventional and traditional approach in view of the ICT environment.

1.2. ICT

ICT is defined as, "Information and Communication Technology, is the technology required for information processing. In particular in the use of electronic computer and computer software to convert, store, protect, process, transmit and retrieve information from anywhere, anytime." It consists of technology such as radio and the newer digital technologies like computers, satellite, mobile phones and the internet. Also it comprises the Electronic collection, editing, storage, distribution and presentation of information.

1.3. Role of ICT in Academic Libraris

Information explosion and the emerging ICT revolution have changed the higher education scenario and the academic libraries to the larger extent. Development and the application of the automation software and implementing the information and communication technologies (ICT) in library operation have changed the traditional activities of the libraries. Libraries are now automated i.e. all the housekeeping operations are now performed by using computers.

ICT is used in libraries and information centers for the development of new information services and computerization of library services. ICT is useful in great extend. It is useful for improving productivity and efficiency of library services effectively. It provides the quality information and also saves the space of the library and save the time of its users. Now a days academic libraries on large scale, utilizing advance scientific ways and know-how and adopting ICT for the best and best practices to cater to the needs of the researchers also accomplish the objectives of the higher education.

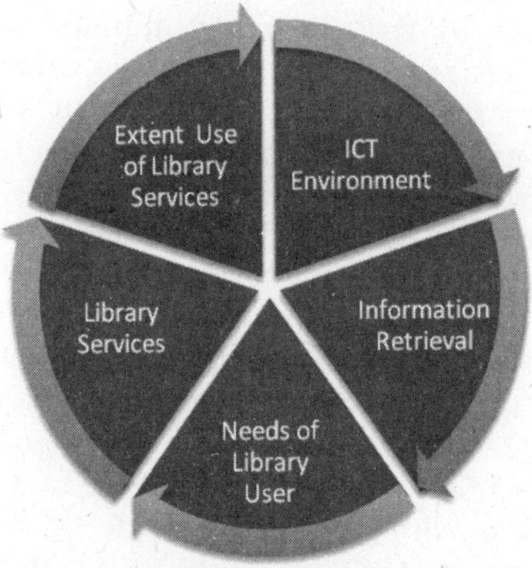

Fig. 1. Impact of ICT Environment. Academic Library

1.4. Commerce College Library

It is a type of special library. The libraries which specialize on certain subjects or group of subjects are called special libraries. A special library is motivated by a particular objective and the collection of material will reflect that objectives.

The special libraries serve a profession, a firm, a research organization, a whole industry, or a single branch of learning. The aim of special library and best qualities of their staff may be similar to those of the university libraries, but they often have little in common; their variety is infinite. They are proposed for limited users with special field of interest.

The Commercial libraries are result of the First World War. The growth of rapid industrialization diverse information technical as well as non-technical was required by the industry and trade without loss of time to solve day to day problems encountered the numerous departments of trade and industry. This resulted in formation of commercial libraries.

The commercial libraries are controlled, financed and managed by the respective industrial concern or business houses. These libraries assist to the organizations in promotion, development and research activities. The commerce librarian besides having basic and ICT based qualifications should have foresight, and should possess through and advanced knowledge of recent affairs in the field of science and technology and World economy, should be competent in transmitting rapid and true services. Much success depends upon the right type of collection in commercial library. Information like encyclopedia, commercial directories, buyer's guides, standard text and reference books, Govt. rules and regulations, patents, standards, trade catalogues, price lists, photographs, charts, etc are to be stocked. In addition to periodicals, journals regarding the trade/ industry, other general of economics and political nature having wide exposure are subscribed.

1.5. BMCC

The Brihan Maharashtra College of Commerce is a pioneering, premier Commerce College in Maharashtra. It was established in 1943 by the Deccan Education Society, Pune with view to provide enlightened leadership and trained manpower in the field of commerce and business which will support to strengthen the economy of our nation. BMCC is the NAAC Accredited "A" Grade College and one of the best commerce academy. It has the glorious history of about 70 years and very proudly continues the rich heritage of the Deccan Education Society.

1.6. BMCC Library

The College has a unique and independent two-storied library building, having total area of about 14500 sq ft. This colossal library building was inaugurated at the hands of late Shri. N. A. Palkhiwala, the eminent jurist of India on the 25th November 1973. It has rare, varied and rich collection. It subscribes to 103 regional, national and international journals. There are 80,000 books available. BMCC Library is recognized today as one of the best and well equipped library in Commerce and Economics. The first Librarian of this library was Pralhad Digambar Kulkarni. During 38 years of his devoted service he developed and organized this library scrupulously. BMCC Library has been growing over the years. Now it has undertaken several measures and adopting modern scientific techniques and know-how to perform day to day tasks. Most of the traditional services have also been replaced by new ICT-based services. This library applying various best practices in providing the best services to its users.

1.7. Present Collection of the Library (TOTAL BOOKs 94,188)

Books

	Series	*No. of Books*
	Sr. College	55040
1	Text Books	4459
2	Junior College	7644
3	Books purchased under UGC Five Year Plan	13992
4	Books purchased under Non-Grant	5867
5	M. Phil Dissertation	352
6	Ph.D. Thesis	226
7	Bound Volumes	6539
8	BRAIL BOOKS:	69

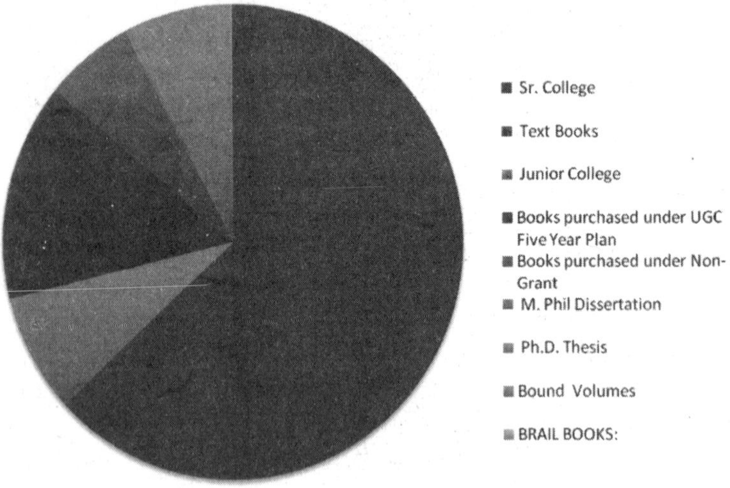

1.8. Library Users

Students of Junior, Senior, PG Wing and teachers of all the faculties also the non- teaching are the regular members of the library. About 4000 students of all the faculties and about 120 teachers availing the services of the library. Ex-teachers, Senior citizens, educationalist and research scholars are visiting the library. As it is one of the leading library in commerce, various persons of banking, trade and economic sector also visited this library from last 40 years.

1.9. Library Staff

The present staff positions of the library are as follows:

The Librarian	1
Asst. Librarian	1
Library Clerk	1
Library Clerk (Non-Grant)	2
Library Attendant	8

1.10. Library Automation

BMCC Library initiated its computerization since 2008. The present automation status of the library is as follows.

1 Libraries Database includes of Books, Periodicals, Theses and new additions.

2 Library has SMART-Lib software to run its computerized functions.

3 About 11 computers are in use for automation work.

4 Installation of OPAC (Online Public Access Catalogue)

5 Installation of Barcode system for Members I-D and Circulation System.

6 Other administrative aspects of the library.

1.11. Library Services

The teachers, research scholars, students and the other staff are the main users of the library. The majority of the under-graduate and post-graduate students depends on the services of the library. For convenience of the readers, the service of the library is made available from 8 am to 5 pm on all working days. Reading- Hall remain open till 8 pm during examination period. Besides the books in the stacks for lending, the library has special collection of textbooks for issue and reference purpose. Reprographic services are provided to the readers on nominal charges to enable them to copy the required materials. The library provides Internet services to the readers for browsing the regular material.

General Services

The general services of the library include:

- General administrative works
- Procurement of information resources to serve the users.
- Infrastructure development in the tune of the demands of the users
- Issue and return of the books, circulation of reference and journal materials and other materials.
- Basic training on the handling of new services as a part of user's education program.
- Reprographic Services and other bindery works
- Stack arrangement and maintenance.
- Provision of up to date information
- Saving time in searching desired information;

Traditional Services

The following traditional library services have been prevailing in the library till date:

- Organization of knowledge resources;
  — Classification following DDC 20th Edition
  — Cataloguing adopting AACR II
- Circulation of reading materials following BROWNE CHARGING SYSTEM;
- Reprographic Service;
- Reading Book Service;

- Reference Service;
- Referral Service;
- News Paper Clipping.
- Inter-library loan / Resource-sharing;
- Book Bank Scheme for deserving students;
- Library Orientation Program;
- Book Exhibition and Lecture series;
- Display of New arrival;
- Night Library facility;
- Research facility for doing research.
- Casual membership for Ex-students

List of Best Practices

New best practices have been introduced in the delivery of services by the library.

- Creation of the databases of the books and other material using library application package like SMART Lib
- Automation of different housekeeping operations of the library.
- Providing OPAC as tool for browsing & searching the library collection.
- Provision of services in electronic environment.
- Developing Local Area Network
- Providing online access to leading E-Journals and E-books to library users/readers at no cost.
- Access to the full text of the journals;
- News Paper Clipping Depository : Scanning the daily news.
- INTERNET & E-Resource Centre providing internet connectivity enabling the users access to global information resources;
- Adopting Barcode System in Circulation and for the

I-Cards & B-T Cards of the library members.

- Joining the INFLIBNET-NList Programme enabling the academic and research community access to more than 6000+ E-Journals and 97000+ E-Books.
- Improving existing service conditions;
- Helping towards promoting E-Learning as well as E-Literacy among the scholars
- Improving the efficiency and effectiveness of the library.
- Making library management more systematic to serve the users conductively.

3. BEST PRACTICES

Innovation and transformation are important concept in today's libraries especially in light of the libraries' ongoing transition from acquiring serials in print to providing access electronically, thus moving toward the virtual library (Carr, 2009). In order for libraries to remain relevant to their customers, they must follow the fundamental rule of business, that is, to supply what is demanded by their market. Library staff skills and library services all have to shift from book-centric to user-centric. As the academic library continues to redefine its role in the digital environment, it needs to leverage its strengths and innovate to create responsive and convenient services (Li, 2006).

In business literature, the importance of involving customers in service innovation and development has been the subject of innovation theory over the last decade or so (e.g. Alam and Perry, 2002; Alam, 2002). For example Bitner et al. (2000) recommend close involvement of customers in the design process of technology-based services.

This paper contributes to the debate on innovation in libraries by particularly focusing on user roles. Other studies have focused on innovation in libraries, but they have taken different perspectives such as employee creativity (Castiglione, 2008), developing knowledge innovation culture in libraries (Sheng and Sun, 2007) or changing customer demands and library's ability to innovate and respond to them (Brindley, 2006; Li, 2006)

1. Computerised Library Services

All activities in the library are done through computer only. All the books have the Bar-code stickers. Students Identity Cards are also Bar-coded. There are & computers having LAN in the library. Out of these two are for library users i.e. for the students and teachers to search the book through OPAC (Online Public Access Catalogue) The task of issuing the books, indexing, reports generation, statistics and section wise computerized library functions and services are become faster and easier due to computerization.

2. Library Membership

Bar-coded and laminated Identity Cards are generated in the library and issued to the students. Through this card they can borrow the books. Library membership cards are also provided to the students to facilitate the issuing. Total of students from Junior wing, UG and PG classes enrolled in the library in the current year.

3. Library Website And E-mail

Library has a separate Website with the Linkage to College website. A user can check any book sitting at home from any corner of the world. *www.bmcclibrary@ vsnl.net* is the name of the website. The E-Mail address of the library is *bmcclibrary12@gmail.com* Users can interact with the library staff through the e-mail for their short term and long term information query and library services.

4. Library User Group

To inculcate the reading habits among the students to encourage them library organizes Library Users Groups. Every year many interested students register their names for LUG. Library Issues a Card to them for extra reading.

5. Institutional Membership

In view to assist the research work and develop the current awareness of the library users, library has taken the institutional membership of the following organization. They provide the important books and information about the recent developments in different subject all over the world.

- MACCIA (Maharashtra Chamber of Commerce, Industry and Agriculture)
- MCCIA (Maratha Chamber of Commerce, Industries and Agriculture)
- BCL (British Council Library, Pune)
- INFLIBNET – N-LIST Program

6. Book Exhibition And Lecture Series

The larger amount of the budget is spent on purchase of books through exhibition. Principal, Professors and students select and recommend the books for purchase. Lecture series has been organized every year along with the books exhibition.

7. Library Orientation Programme

Library arranges the Orientation Program twice a week. To acquaint the students about the library rules, collection and services. It helps them to know the library, its information sources, searching tools and facilities thoroughly.

8. Free Neternet And E-resournce Centre

There is a well equipped computer lab comprising

20 computers. Library provides internet facility to all students free of cost. Due to this magnificent computer lab the traditional appearance of the library has been changed thoroughly. It has become the knowledge hub for library users. They can browse and access worldwide information through the internet facility. Near about 80 students surf the universal information every day. They can read online databases, online journals, full text current information sources. There is overwhelming response from students community for this facility.

9. Book Bank Scheme

There is a 'Book Bank Scheme' for the needy and deserving students of all classes. A set of text-books is issued to the students for the whole academic year. Students avail this unique library facility and a number of students apply for this scheme every year.

10. Reference And Referral Service

Library provides the long-term and short-term reference service to all its readers. Reference desk deals with all sort of authentic and important reference books, dictionaries, manuals, directories, indexes, annuals. All types of queries are promptly responded through reference desk.

11. Display of New Arrival

Library periodically displays the newly purchased books and journals for the readers. This is to inform the readers about newly published books journals. List of newly added books is displayed every month for students and faculty.

12. Book Discount Scheme

Every year the college gives a special Book Discount to students for purchasing new books from the book exhibition. There is overwhelming response from the students for this scheme.

13. Night Library

Reading-Hall of the library remains open till 8.00 pm during examinations. Students take the advantage of this library service on large scale. More than 500 students avail the facility every day.

14. Inter-library Loan

Library exchanging its information sources with the leading libraries in Pune City. Research, academic and university libraries like BJ Wadia Library of Fergusson College, Jaykar Library of University of Pune, Library of Bhandarkar Institute, etc's are sharing its information sources with our library.

15. Study Cubicals for Teachers

For teaching- staff members the arrangement of study cubicles has been made in the Library. A computer with internet is provided. They can browse the INFLIBNET-NLIST and other online journals and full text information sources for their do research.

16. Digitized News-paper-clipping Service

Scanning, classifying and organizing the daily national and international news regarding trade, commerce, banking and economic sector is an important service provided by the library to its users. News paper clippings provide the latest and current information in trade and commerce. It is the Current Awareness Service which keeps the users informed about the Governments new polices, rules and regulations, fluctuations in the Nation and International trade, market and economy. Students and teachers ask for this information frcquently.

17. Dissertation, Thesis and Reports

Library has preserved valuable collection of M. Phil. and Ph. D. theses since 1985. There are near about 352 M. Phil. dissertations and about 226 Ph. D. thesis arranged in the library, which is now properly organized and listed in OPAC. Researchers and students can refer to these important information sources.

18. N-List Programe

Library has subscribed to INFLIBNET N-LIST PROGRAME. There are 97000 leading national and international e-journals and 6000 e-books are available full text. Library users are provided the USERID and the PASSWORD to search, brows , refer or to down load the articles of their interest. This gives a very comprehensive and most recent information of different area of knowledge.

19. OPAC (Online Public Access Catalogue)

Every single document, print and non-print is entered in the OPAC. Users can search their title in the OPAC. This Online Public Access Catalogue is an important tool for searching the exact source of information preserved and organized in the library. Various options are provided to search the title i.e. Author, Title, Publisher, Accession Number, Keywords etc. Users find it very convenient and time saving to locate their title through OPAC.

20. Competitive Exam Section

There are near about 108 books related to MPSC, UPSC, NET, SET, CET and other competitive examination acquired and kept in special section for the concerned students and the teachers preparing for the exams.

CONCLUSIONS

The above state of circumstances presents the current status of the BMCC Library. With the introduction of new best practices, the mode of delivery of services of library has changing. Users are really taking advantage of these new practices in the library services. BMCC Library is serving as model for commerce college academic libraries. Technology alone cannot help bring about the required changes. Attitudes, practices, and policies need to change if libraries are to truly benefit themselves and their community of users by the application of new technologies.

REFRENCES

- Kulkarni, H.Y., 'The Annals of Deccan Education Society's Brihan Mhyarashtra College of Commerce,Pune' Diamond Jubilee Publication (1943-2004), 2004, pp. 73-76.
- Lanjekar, J. Ed., 'Arthavyavahar', BMCC, Pune, 2009-2012.
- Kumar, K. (2001). *Reference Services*. N.Delhi: Vikas P.House.
- Ranganadham, D. S. (2013, May 25/10/2013). Qualities of Library Professionals in ICT Environment. Tirupati, India.
- Ranganadham, D. S. (2013, May). Qualities of Library Professionals in ICT Environment. *Indian Journal of Applied Research* , pp. 366-367.
- Salam, V., & Singh, I. S. (2007). Best Practices in Library Services: A case Study of Manipur University Library. *5th Convention Planner-2007* (pp. 154-159). Gauhati: Gauhati University.
- Scupola, A., & Nicolajsen, H. W. (2010). Service Innovation In Academic Libraries: Is There a Place for the Customers? . *Forthcoming In Library Management* , pp. 304-318.
- *www.http//wikipedia.* (n.d.). Retrieved August 28, 2013, from http://www.wikipedia
- Brindley, L. (2006) "Re-defining the library", Library Hi Tech, Bradford, Vol. 24, No. 4; pg. 484 Li, X. (2006), "Library as incubating space for innovations: practices, trends and skill sets", Library Management, Bradford, Vol. 27, Nos. 6/7; pg. 370-378.
- Alam, I. and Perry, C. (2002), "A customer-oriented new service development process", Journal of Services Marketing, Vol.16, No. 6, pp.515-534.
- Bitner, M. J., Brown, S. W. and Meuter, M. L. (2000), "Technology infusion in service encounter", Journal of the Academy of Marketing Science, Vol.28, No. 1, pp. 138-149

7

Best Practices of Chandmal Tarachand Bora College Library & Information Centre

Shantashree Sengupta
Librarian & Head, Department of Library & Information Science, Chandmal Tarachand Bora Arts, Commerce & Science College Shirur, Dist.Pune.

ABSTRACT

Impact of Information Communication & Technology (ICT) can be very well witnessed in the overall functioning of academic libraries. Considering the importance of Library and Information Centre in the development of an academic institution, UGC, NAAC, State and Central Government has planned various schemes for the advancement and promotion of library services. Libraries play a crucial role in the institutional accreditation since they largely support learning, teaching and research activities in the institution. In this paper the researcher lists the various best practices adopted by the C.T.Bora College Library.

Keywords : Best Practices, C.T.Bora College Library, NAAC

INTRODUCTION

"Libraries Store the Energy that fuels the imagination. They open up winds to the world and inspire us to explore and achieve and contribute to improving our quality of life. Libraries change lives for the better."

— ***Sidney Sheldon***

The above quote by Sidney Sheldon presents a clear image of library, the expectations that users have from libraries, services provided by the libraries etc. Libraries are definitely powerhouse of knowledge. Librarian and other staff of libraries are expected to introduce the users to almost all the sources of information available in the library and sometimes beyond that. The information contained in the books, journals etc. urge the user to explore to many more sources of information. Libraries in a way change the lives of the user community by changing the way in which a person looks into a concept, a topic. The advent of information communication and technology helped the new age libraries to break the boundaries of information access and provide the user easy access to information available in libraries of the same city/ state/ nation/world.

The history of higher education in India proves that Radhakrishnan (1948) and Kothari (1964) Commission Reports have already recognized the role of libraries in higher education. They had recommended the need of a first class library for the college and universities. Moreover UGC Library Committee Report (1965) headed by Dr. S.R. Ranganathan provided firm base to academic libraries. INFLIBNET since its inception in 1989 has been providing financial support to the academic libraries to automate library operations. Today INFLIBNET claims that it has supported more than 150 universities for library automation. It is hoped that within a decade almost all the universities will have library automation.

Library and Information Services of Higher Education institutions play a central role in enhancing the quality of academic and research environment. Keeping in view the importance of libraries in higher education various organizations of national importance like UGC/ NAAC/ AICTE have framed polices or guidelines defining the essential requirements and guidelines to set up a proper academic library. National

Knowledge Commission Report (2007) also realizes the significance or the role of different types of libraries. University Grants Commission (UGC) , The apex body of higher education in India, created a higher education body , NAAC (National Assessment & Accreditation Council) in 1994 in Bangalore on the recommendation of National Policy of Education (NPE) in 1986.

The National Accreditation and Assessment Council (NAAC) strive for quality and excellence in higher education and advocates for enhancing the role of Library and Information Services in improving academic environment. Document prepared by NAAC for "Best Practices in Academic Libraries says : "Best practice may be innovative and be a philosophy, policy, strategy, program, process or practice that solves a problem or create new opportunities and positively impact on organizations. NAAC developed a set of best practices followed in academic libraries and presented under the following four broad areas:

1. MANAGEMENT AND ADMINISTRATION OF A LIBRARY

- In-service Programmes
- Observation of other Library practice.
- Staff promotional policy.
- Maintenance of service area
- Special deposit scheme
- Resource Generation through external membership.
- Resource generation through internet services.
- Student participation programme.

2. COLLECTION AND SERVICES

- Collection development in different formats
- Compact storage of less used collection
- Library book exhibition
- Extended library opening hours

- Extended hours of service

3. EXTENT OF USE OF SERVICES

- User education Initiation to freshers
- Preparatory course for students project
- User orientation Information aids
- Library use statistics
- Library best user award
- User feedback practice through different formats
- Suggestion box and timely response

4. USE OF TECHNOLOGY IN LIBRARIES

- On-line information retrieval- Internet access
- Free browsing unit -Internet access.
- Broadband internet centre
- Library homepage for information dissemination
- A strong and dynamic library website
- User feedback through library homepage
- Access to e-resources
- Information retrieval through web OPAC
- Campus-wide LAN facility
- Database creation using international standard formats
- Electronic surveillance system CCTV

For college libraries NAAC has developed the following set of best practices for college libraries:

1) Computerization of library with standard software.
2) Inclusion of sufficient information about the library in the college prospectus.
3) Compiling student / teacher statistics
4) Displaying newspaper clippings and a clipping file maintained periodically.
5) Career/ employment information services

6) Internet facility to different user groups
7) Information literacy programmes
8) Suggestion Box
9) Displaying New Arrivals
10) Conduct book exhibition on different occasions
11) Organizing book talks
12) Instituting Annual Best Use Award for students
13) Organizing competitions annually
14) Conduct user survey periodically

Vyas (2009) commented that the above set of best practices for college libraries prepared by NAAC cannot be termed as the last word. The following set of practices too should have been included in it.

1) Making of a Path Finder to the library
2) Keeping the library premises neat and clean
3) Compiling a list of Current Serials/ catalogue of journals.
4) Updating and maintaining library website
5) Maintaining useful statistics regarding the use of the library and displaying them on the library walls
6) Compiling checklists on different subject/topics as a part of documentation service
7) Library Committee formation
8) Distribution of useful handouts

Meaning of 'Best Practices'

According to Bogan & English (1994), "A best practice is a method or technique that has consistently shown results superior to those achieved with other means, and that is used as a benchmark. In addition, a "best" practice can evolve to become better as improvements are discovered. Best practices are used to maintain quality as an alternative to mandatory legislated standards and can be based on self-assessment or benchmarking."

ODLIS (Online Dictionary of Library and Information Science) describes best practices as follows: "In the application of theory to real-life situations, procedures that, when properly, applied consistently yield superior results and are therefore used as reference points in evaluation of the effectiveness of alternative methods of accomplishing the same task. Best practices are identified by examining empirical evidence of success."

Review of Literature

Raut (2013) attempted to study the best practices in accredited academic libraries of Sant Gadge Baba Amravati University Region and found that the libraries before accreditation have less weightage, only 10 % College libraries are well developed, but after NAAC Accreditation process almost all libraries try to look toward library development. The most effective part in Accreditation is Best Practices and if all follow the best practices then it will help in increasing the effectiveness of the service/ department/ process.

Umesh (2012) throw light with the introduction to the role of academic libraries and the impact of ICT on them in the present context. The paper stresses on the current challenges faced by the academic libraries, and how they can be overcome by using the best practices. The paper emphasizes on the fact that the adoption of the best practices in academic libraries will help in continuous improvement and overall performance in the institution / organization.

Wadje (2012) mentioned that as per NAAC guidelines the Indira Gandhi Senior College Library, Nanded adopted various best practices in its administration, management, collection & services, extent of the use of services and use of technology. The documentation on the best practices followed in the IGSC

Library will initiate other libraries to opt for the ideal way of managing the libraries and services of academic institutions.

Kamble & Tikam (2011) state that to cope with the timely challenges, every library has to identify and develop its own tailor-made best practices to enhance the collection development process, services dissemination and use of the library as a whole. Appropriate planning, fore thinking, a detailed analysis of user base, objectives of the affiliating institution and its future strategies should be taken into account while planning any best practice. Developing best practices, analyzing and revising them at a regular interval will lead to continuous improvement in overall performance of the library and the whole institution.

Vyas (2009) provides UGC's data about universities, colleges, teachers and students which have grown over a period of last 58 years and defined best practices as an application of procedures to yield superior results. It explained NAAC's concern for quality of library practices as well as NAAC's set of best practices in academic libraries. The paper provides a few examples of the best practices experienced in libraries in different situations by Indian library scientists like Dr. S.R. Ranganathan and others. It elaborates upon Prof. Tikekar's comment that blind imitation, false competition, status symbolism will not work and finally submits that best practices of British libraries and American Center Libraries operating in India should be followed for our libraries too.

About Shirur Shikshan Prasarak Mandal (SSPM)

Shirur Shikshan Prasarak Mandal was established by eminent social workers and some of the then government officers in 1945 with main objective to establish secondary schools for the rural children. SSPM is presently working in four talukas of Pune and Ahmednagar District with one primary school (English/

Marathi medium), eight high schools, six junior colleges, one senior college and one management institute. This academic expansion was possible only because of the dedicated services rendered by the trustees, teachers and other staff of schools and colleges. The governing council of SSPM is non-political and too much supportive body for the expansion of education to the lowest strata of the society. All the academic units of SSPM have reached to the height of excellence in the field of academics and proved it in different merit list of state board and university exams.

About the College

Shirur Shikshan Prasarak Mandal's Chandmal Tarachand Bora Arts, Commerce and Science College was established in 1968. This was then only centre for higher studies in the draught prone area of Pune and Ahmednagar District of Maharashtra. During the last five decades (46 years) college has developed itself as one of the most reputed centre for higher studies and proud feel college affiliated to Savitribai Phule Pune University, Pune. The College has been re-accredited by NAAC with 'A' Grade in January 2013. The College has received the prestigious 'Best College Award 2014-15' by Savitribai Phule Pune University, Pune.

The college is named after Chandmal Tarachand Bora who was a great supporter of education in Shirur. This was the first centre of higher learning in the vicinity which is mainly a draught prone area where major section of the society was economically weak and educationally backward. Limited agricultural production was the only source of income for these families. Because of the weak economic condition and education backwardness, students did not turn up to the college in large number in the first three decades. The Governing Council Members of C.T.Bora College and teachers of the college have taken utmost pain to reach to the commonest person in the area to enroll the students in the initial days. Since the last two decades, there is an enthusiastic response of the students and at present more than 3000 students have enrolled in the college for various UG and PG programmes.

C.T.Bora College Library & Information Centre

Along with the academic and sports facilities, college has well stacked library spread in 11, 000 sq.ft. The library has been the '*heart of the institution*' since its inception. It has separate Reading Hall for Boys and Girls, Reading Hall for PG & Research Students and Faculty Members. The Library has also maintained separate Stacking Sections for Undergraduate, Post-Graduate and Research. The library maintains a good collection of reference books, theses, dissertation, Minor and Major Project Reports of Faculties, Project Reports of UG and PG Students etc.

Library has subscription to INFLIBNET's N-LIST E-resources, has UGC-Network Resource Centre and provides Reprographic Facility to its users. Recently the library has started barcode project for all the library books and plans to digitize and reserve some of the books for longtime access through online mode. The library provides Wi-fi facility which provides uninterrupted Internet Connectivity to the users on their laptop/ Tablets/ Smartphones etc.

The library also has separate Audio-Visual Hall which has TV, Computer, LCD, DVD Player and is generally used by the faculty members for imparting teaching with the help of audio-visual resources.

Library & Information Centre – As Learning Resource

Sr. No.	*Item*	*Number*
1	Total No. of Books (Volumes)	78000+
2	Total No. of Titles	50021
3	Journals Subscribed	26

4	Periodicals/Magazines Subscribed	34
5	Total No. of E-Journals (Accessible by INFLIBNET'S N-LIST)	5000+
6	Bound Volumes	505
7	No. of Video-Cassettes	154
8	No. of Cds	548
9	No. of Computers	10
10	Internet Connectivity, Wi-fi	10 Mbps Broadband

The library automation work is started using 'Vriddhi Office Automation Software' developed by Hindustan Computers, Malegaon, Dist.Nasik few years back. The library has purchased Barcode Label Printer which helps in expediting the process of barcoding of books.

Other than the College Library Budget, with the financial assistance received from UGC under various Plan Grants and Special Schemes, the library could acquire costly reference books required for various PG and Research Centres. In order to ensure proper expenditure of budget, the Library has constituted two separate committees for monitoring the overall working. They are:

(a) Library Committee : The committee mainly sanctions the library budget for the Academic Year, administers the overall functioning of the library, discusses issues related to new services to be introduced, purchase of equipments required for the library, staff issues, user suggestions etc.

(b) Book Purchase Committee : The committee monitors the proper expenditure of College Budget and UGC Library Budget throughout the year for both the semesters, approves the purchase of books depending on the requirement, demand and budget availability of the concerned department.

During NAAC Accreditation and Re-Accreditation Peer Team visits, Savitribai Phule Pune University (Pune)

'Best College' Inspection team Visit, and regular visits of members of various Committees, Conference Participants, the library and information centre receives lots of appreciation due to its collection, maintenance, facilities and services provided and the dedication of library staff which was visible from the user satisfaction towards the library.

Best Practices adopted by the Library & Information Centre are:

1. Meetings of Library Committee and Book Purchase Committee Meetings are conducted at regular intervals which help in proper budget expenditure, purchase of books and journals, and overall maintenance of library.
2. Orientation Programme is organized in the library. In the beginning of the academic year, the faculty members bring the students in small groups to the library wherein they are introduced to Library resources, Library Rules and Regulations and Library Services.
3. Regular book exhibitions are organized in the library during various conferences/ seminars or special events which are kept open for the faculties and the students.
4. New books purchased by the library are displayed in the 'New Arrivals Display' at regular intervals. This makes the library user aware of the new books added to the collection.
5. With the help of the UGC-Network Resource Centre (UGC-NRC), the library is able to provide 10Mbps Broadband Internet connectivity to the students.
6. The library also provides Wi-fi facility which enables the users to access e-resources in their Smartphones, iPad, Laptop etc.
7. Online assistance is provided to the users to download information from the Internet.

8. In the beginning of every academic year, the College conducts ICT Workshop for teaching and non-teaching faculty members. In this workshop, special sessions are engaged by the librarian to make the teaching faculty members aware of the online search strategies, use of N-LIST, knowledge of free e-resources across various disciplines etc.

   The non-teaching faculty members are also trained regarding the use of ICT for their administrative work like searching Government Resolutions, searching information from websites of University, Govt. of Maharashtra, and Social Welfare etc.

   Such workshops helped the faculty members to increase use of ICT in teaching and administrative work thereby performing their duties in more effective and efficient manner.

9. Reprographic facility is provided to the students in the library.

10. Till date, the Library & Information Centre has successfully organized 01 National Conference Sponsored by UGC, 01 National Conference and 01 District Level Seminar sponsored by BCUD, Savitribai Phule Pune University. All the conferences received overwhelming response from the participants who contributed their research papers for the Conference Proceedings. In this way, the library gives an opportunity to its students as well as provides a healthy professional platform for other library professionals to exchange their views, ideas and to learn from the stalwarts in the field.

11. Book-bank facility is provided for needy students. Physically handicapped students are issued the academic books on yearly basis.

12. Inter-library loan facility is provided as per requirement.

13. Students under Earn and Learn Scheme work in the various sections of library.
14. Newspaper Clippings Service is provided.
15. Library Security is taken care of by continuous monitoring with the help of CCTVs installed in the library.
16. The library has a special collection of books for Coaching of NET/SET/SLET and for Entry in Services. Remedial Coaching assistance is also provided by the library. These Sections are developed with the help of financial assistance received from UGC, New Delhi.
17. The library helps the PG Departments and Research Centres to develop their Departmental Libraries.
18. 'Table of Contents' Service is provided by the library. The Table of Contents of Journals is scanned and mailed to the Heads of the Department regularly.
19. Important news related to education, university, book reviews, articles are displayed on the library notice board as wells as on the College General Notice Board.
20. Every day in the last working hour, shelving of the books, cleaning of shelves and library area is done.

CONCLUSION

The changing trends in work environment have made it important for the library and information professionals to develop and follow certain Best Practices in order to provide quality services to the users. Keeping in accordance with the 'Best Practices in Academic Library' developed by NAAC, all the academic libraries have introduced several new services by involving ICT and other modern technologies.

While framing and implementing the best practices for our library we all should remember and keep into consideration the available staff, resources, user community, budgetary provisions etc. It is very important to understand that the best practices suitable for one library may not deliver similar results for another library. The librarian and other library staff should perform their regular duties in the best possible way in order to achieve the goals of the library and to satisfy the user community. Instead of following some other institution's 'Best Practices', the practices adopted by us should bridge the gap between the library and the users for effective and maximum utilization of the resources, which will result in the development and up gradation of higher educational goals and the vision and mission of the library and the institution at large.

REFERENCES

1. *Best Practices-Library & Information Services: A Case Presentation.* Retrieved 16th January 2015 from *http://www.naac.gov.in/best_practices.asp*
2. Bogan, C.E. and English, M.J.(1994). *Benchmarking for Best Practices: Winning Through Innovative Adaptation.* New York: McGraw-Hill.
3. Definition of Best Practices. Retrieved 15th January 2015 from *http://www.abc-clio.com/ODLIS/odlis_b.aspx*
4. Kamble A, & Tikam, M (2011). *Best Practices in Academic Libraries.* Version 2. *LIS Compendium.* Retrieved January 30th, 2015from: *https://liscompendium. wordpress.com/article/best-practices-in-academic-libraries-35muq6i9t1aro-3/.*
5. Raut, A.S. & Kokate, R.G. (2013). Study of Best Practices in the Accredited Academic Libraries of Sant Gadge Baba Amravati University region. Retrieved February 1st, 2015 from *www.inflibnet.ac.in/caliber2013/ppt/1_11.pptx*
6. Umesh, K. Y. (2012). Best practices adopted in academic libraries and information resource centres. *International Journal of Information Dissemination and Technology, 2*(3), 186-188. Retrieved January 20th, 2015 from *www.ijidt.com/index.php/ijidt/article/download/198/91*
7. Vyas, S.D. (2009). *Best Practices in Academic Libraries in India: A Study.* Retrieved January 15th, 2015 from *http://*

www.libsys.co.in/download/best%20practices_in_india_libraries.pdf

8. Wadje, K.N. (2012). Best Practices in Library of Indira Gandhi Senior College (IGSC), Nanded. *Research Vistas, 1*(2),97-107. Retrieved 1st February, 2015 from *http://egranthalaya.nic.in/16Kailas.pdf*

8

Best Practices in the Library : A Case Study of DGT College Library

Jagdish Vyas
Research Scholar, SRTMU, Nanded
Dahifale Vikram
R.M.I.G.College, Jalna

ABSTRACT

The paper explain best practices implemented by D. G. Tatkare Arts & Commerce Library, Tala for serving library user.

Keywords : Best practices, DGT library

INTRODUCTION

Best, perfect, wonderful, great, mind blowing, excellent, prime, superb, etc. are the terms that always catch human attention. That is because human race has great fascination for best. The meaning of best varies from time to time, person to person and even from place to place. Today's best may not be tomorrows best. Similarly something best for one person may not be best for the other. Something considered best at one place may not be best at other place. Libraries are starving always for the best depends on their location and user because libraries are serving people Library plays an important role in enhancing & sustaining the quality of higher education. Best practices are introducing new ideas, techniques in order to improve quality or to make progress. Librarian should make all attempt to over come such resistance from staff as well as user to change, once the best practices should be monitored and review continuously. Best practices should meet or Exide the need and expectations of the user as best practice may be innovative & be a philosophy, strategy, program, proceeds or practice that solve a problem, or create new opportunities. It may be potential. It is the practice which paves the wave for enhancing & existing function, & helps in effective implementation or use for the process.

PROFILE OF THE COLLEGE : D. G.TATKARE ARTS & COMMERCE COLLEGE, TALA

D.G.Tatkare Arts and Commerce College is a leading college affiliated to Mumbai University. It was established in 2001 by Tale Vibhag Shikshan Prasarak Mandal, Tale trust with a number of academic institutions, under its umbrella. In 2001 only Art faculty was stared in senior college. In 2003, Commerce faculty was started in senior college to fulfill the higher educational needs of the students. The College has earned laurels in the field of academics, as well as in extra and co-curricular activities. College has a long list of distinguished alumni. College have represented at the State Level and National Level and have won many trophies and championships. College have been running add on courses in computer from 2009. From academic year 2013-2014 College has got permission from State Government to start Post graduate courses of Master of Commerce (M.Com) and Master of Art (Political Science).

NAAC accreditated to college with B grade & CGPA of 2.45 during Feb. 2014.

College library is established in 2001. It is

computerized with e-Granthalaya library automation software. Library reading room has seating arrangement for 40 students. Reading room is available to students from 7.00 a.m. to 4.00 p.m. Internet facility is given to user to use e-resources.

BEST PRACTICES OF THE LIBRARY

D.G.Tatkare Arts & Commerce College Library have been implemented following concept as best practices to serve library user. Because of these concept user frequency of visit to the library & use of library resources increased. These practices are actual services of the library.

Library Automation

e-Granthalaya software of National Information Center, Delhi is used as a Library Management Software. Barcode enabled borrow card has been given to all user of the library. It saves book issue / return time of the user. It also knows details of transaction of Books during search period.

OPAC

Library used e-Granthalaya software for

Automation. It has facility of OPAC (Online Public Access Catalogue). One computer terminal is provided in the library for OPAC services. User can search books availability & details of books in the library.

WEBOPAC

e-Granthalaya software is integrated with National Information Centre, Delhi. Students can see library collections & availability of books on the website http://egranthalaya.nic.in.

Library Website

Library has its website http://www.dgtlibrarytala.webs.com which includes library rules, timing, news, notices, list of collections, link to college website, link to access resources on publishers website & university website also. College website dgtcollegetala.org has a link to library portal.

Digital Library (Institutional Repositories)

D-Space software is used as an institutional repositories. Repositories contains University Question Papers, syllabus, e-books & articles. Four Computers are provided to use these resources.

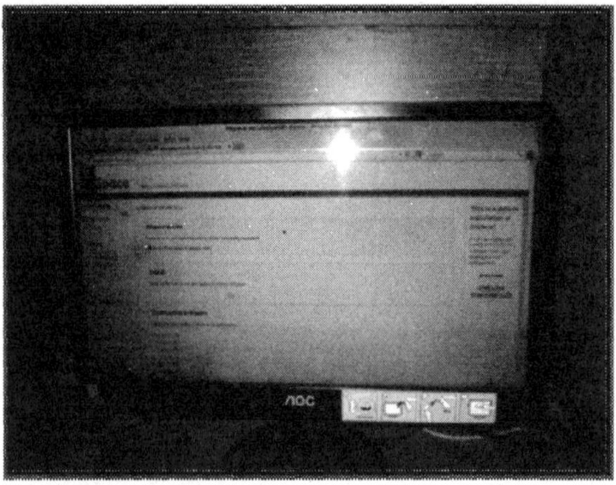

Interlibrary Loan (ILL)

Library made MOU with D.R.Deshmukh Public Libray, Tala, G. M. Vedak College of Science, Tala, G.M. Vedak High School & Jr. College, Tala & D.G. Tatkare Mahavidyalaya, Mangaon for sharing of their collections through Interlibrary Loan Scheme.

Earn & Learn Scheme

Students are working in library under earn & learn scheme. They have improved their knowledge by learning library work & its collections.

Book Exhibition

Book exhibition of Books of Yashwantrao Chavan Maharashtra Open University, Nashik & Marathi General Books in the library are performed by the Library. Every year library have been organising book exhibition display week. Book collection of Political Science, Geography, Economics, Marathi & Commerce subject in the library are displayed in book exhibition during celebration of display week by the library.

Book Bank Scheme

One set of Text books is given among three or four student under Book bank scheme for one term.

Reprography

Reprography facility is given to students on nominal charges. One Xerox Machine in Office & one printer in library are made available for it.

Manuscript

Topper students last years answer books & hand written good project report, teachers notes & their articles are valuable asset of college. Hence these are kept under manuscript section of the library for reference.

Career News

Informative articles regarding interview procedure & techniques, various vocational courses & employment news are displayed under career forum.

New Arrivals

List of new books arrived in the library is displayed on notice board.

Sometimes new book front rapper is displayed.

Today's Word

To make familiar with one English word every day, one word in English with their meaning in Marathi is displayed everyday on Library Notice Board.

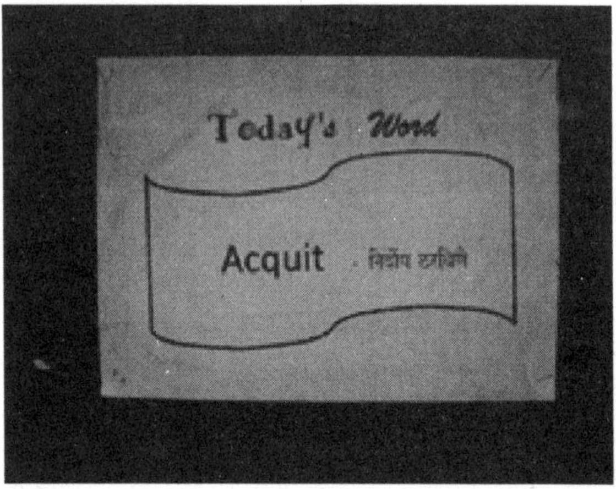

Bibliography

Bibliography of Publisher, subject wise bibliography, bibliography of books in nearby libraries & bibliography of Braille books are compiled to know about information of books available in the market.

User Orientation / awareness program

User orientation & awareness program is initiated for new user to know about use of OPAC, How to use N-LIST & classification of books in the library.

News Paper

Daily news papers are displayed on two news paper stand, one kept in the library & another in the students reading room.

News paper Clipping

News paper Clipping project on subjects - career

news, general knowledge, speaking tree article in Times of India & informative articles are compiled for reference to students. One month course on News paper clipping, editing & binding is also organised by library.

Braille Books

Braille books on fiction, poem, story, grammar, encyclopedia & Hindi Calendar are kept for blind students. These books are made available to blind people in Tala Taluka.

N-LIST

College is a member of N-LIST (Online Database of National Library & Information Services for Scholarly Content) online database of INFLIBNET. User ID & Password are provided to each students and staff by INFLIBNET. Four Computer terminal with internet facility is given by the library for accessing online resources.

Book Review Competition

To increase reading habit among students book review competition organized for all students.

Open Access

Open access system is implemented in the library. Students are searching their book directly from stack.

Suggestion Box

Suggestion Box is provided in the library for students to put their suggestion for improvement in the library services.

Feedback Form

Every year feedback form is filled by library from the students. Data in these form are analysed. Findings of these data are displayed in graphical form on notice board. Weak services of library are improved by analysis of feedback report.

Book Talk

Students are selected to take part in discussion on a specific book and script reading session arranged on a current published book.

Reader Club

Reader club is formed in tala town containing some students member & some member of public library. Discussion on new arrivals & books read are main points of sharing during club meeting.

Best Reader Award

To attract more students to visit the library & use the resources, best reader award is given to the student. Based on the circulation data & observation of the library staff one best user award is given to the students who has made maximum use of the library. The award in the form of cash/book is given to best user.

Competitive Exam Center

Library provides various competitive exam books & magazine to user. Advertise of competitive exam published in news paper are displayed on notice board. Test exam are conducted by the center. Lecture of eminent persons are arranged to students for guidance.

Internet Service

Today internet is the fast way of dissemination of information & main stream of e- resources. Free internet service access is provided to students to use e- resources, NLIST database & various informative website.

Class room teaching by librarian

Librarian is taking lecture in the class to teach basic information of library & resources available & its uses.

CONCLUSION

DGT College library provides range of best practices to user because of it NAAC accreditation committee was given good remark under criteria of learning resources. The documentation on the best practices followed in the selected libraries will initiate other libraries to opt for the ideal way of managing the libraries and services of academic institutions. With the global village concept, the academic libraries need to orient to the highly qualitative information collection and services. The current networked environment enables the libraries to outreach any users at remote locations. Thus the libraries need to be dynamic and' extend their services beyond the traditional ones, which were confined to book and other print collections. The best practices outlined in the document will be reviewed periodically and the up to date policies and practices will be framed. We do hope that this basic document would initiate the best practices in the Indian academic libraries.

REFERENCES

1. Kumbahr,B.D. (2013), 'Validating best for modern librarianship by Rudyard Kipling's Six honest servants' in Changing Paradigm of Academic Libraries in the E-Environment', Seva Sadan college of Education, Ulhasnagar
2. Kulkarni, S.A. Best Practices in College Libraries. National Seminar on Library and Information Services in Changing Era, 22-23 January 2009. p. 273-281.
3. Mokashi, R.M. Best Practices in Librarianship- Services to the readers : Compilations of Who's Who. National Seminar on Library and Information Services in Changing Era. 22-23 January 2009. p. 285-294.
4. NAAC: A Profile. Bangalore, National Assessment and Accreditation Council, 2006. A Brochure
5. NAAC. Best Practices in Library and Information Services. (Website) Library and Information Services: Case Presentations. NAAC, 2006.
6. Vyas, S. D. (2009) Best Practices in Academic Libraries in India: A Study. In: proceeding of International Conference on Academic Library. 2009, 5th-8th Oct.. India, New Delhi. Delhi University Library System, University of Delhi.

9

Best Practices in Ness Wadia College of Commerce Library Pune

Manojkumar Thakur
Librarian, M.Com. M.Lib. & I. Sc., SET

Surekha R. Khare
Assistant Librarian, M.Com. M.Lib. & I. Sc., NET, SET

ABSTRACT

Best practices are the result of creativity and passion to provide the best services to the users within limited resources and manpower. The internet and web has created certain challenges before academic libraries. The biggest challenge before library is the underutilization of resources. This paper is about the best practices adopted by Ness Wadia College library to inculcate reading habits, adaptation of suitable ICT base best practices and marketing of library services and preparation of NAAC Visit.

Key Words: Best practice, Marketing of library services

1. INTRODUCTION

The sole objective of any library is to fulfill the information needs of its user. The main function of the library is collection, preservation and dissemination of knowledge; make possible efforts to achieve the goals and objectives of parent's organization by providing library services. Therefore it is essential to design and developed library services which will assure optimum utilization of available resources. In the era of Internet and Web Technology, ocean of information is available to the users. Users give first preference to search information on the internet and then visit the library. In an e-environment the role of librarian becomes very crucial. They have to design and develop strategy to provide the information which is at par in the same community. Libraries have shown great flexibility to adopt the new technology to solved their problem and enable them to provide best services. In the present time it is highly essential to practice professionalism and enhance the goodwill of the LIS fraternity .Libraries has to prove their usefulness to the academic community by providing best possible services to them. They have to market the library services and treat the students' community as customer.

2. OBJECTIVES

Best practices are the probable solution to the various problems faced by the library at different occasion. The objectives of all best practices adopted in library are as under

- To enhance the quality of library services by adopting suitable ICT equipment and software.

- To overcome the Problem of acute shortage of manpower in the library
- To eliminate the problem of bad hand writing.
- To assured uniformity and accuracy in technical process.
- To avoid the wastage of stationary
- To save the time of the library staff and users
- To attract the students to the library
- To encourage the students to read more books other than syllabus.

3. COLLEGE PROFILE

The Ness Wadia College of Commerce was established on 15th July 1969.

Courses Offered and annual intake of Students

S. No.	*Particulars*	*Courses*	*Intake*
1	Undergraduates	XI and XII	1741
2	Degree Courses	B.com,	2322
3	Degree Courses	BBA, BBM(IB), BCA,MCA	1065
4	Post Graduate Courses	M.Com I and II	238
5	Post Graduate Diplomas	PGDTL, PGDIB, PG Diploma in Banking and Finance	214
6	Research Students	PhD.	19
7	Faculty	Senior/Junior/Non-Grant	76
8	Administrative Staff	Grant/Non-grant	68
	Total	5743	

3.1. Library

A college library well equipped with books and other resources. Our goal throughout has been to strive for excellence and each day we take a step forward in time and near to our goal that is to provide reading material to our faculty and student, ultimately resulting to fulfill our institute goal that is to impart Commerce and Business Education to the young generation of India.

Library's Stock of Reading Material

Sr. No.	*Particulars*	*Total*
1	Books	51801
2	Journals	103
3	Newspapers	21
4	Bound Volumes	2001
5	Thesis/Dissertation/Project Reports	93/36/85
6	Audio-visual Material	354
7	E-resources	N-list

3.2. Best Practices

Library has started library automation process by using SOUL LIBRARY SOFTWARE Developed by UGC INFLIBNET CENTRE, Ahmadabad. At present library uses latest version of Soul Library Software 2.0. Ness Wadia college of Commerce Pune Library has adopted best practices such as

3.2.1. ICT Based Best Practices

1. Content Page Service: Content page of book service is provided by Ness Wadia College Library. The library have acquired Cannon Cano Scan 5600F Scanner which has the facility to scan multiple pages .The library is scanning title and content page of selected books. The library software SOUL 2.0, cataloguing module has an attachment facility. Where one can attach an attachment of scan images of title and content page of the books and one can see the scan images while searching the OPAC.

2. In House Computerized Book Card Printing System: Computerized book card printing software is purchased for the library. With the help of a canon Pixma MP 150 printer, book cards are printed on the blank book card. Computer generated book card system can produce as many as book cards having college logo with library name, author, title, accession number and barcode of accession number. This facilitate speedy issue of books.

3. In-house Barcode Printing System: ARGOX Barcode printer is purchased for library to print various types of barcode. The library is also generating spine labels in different sizes and numbers, it also helps shelving staff to search books speedily and avoid problem of feint and bad handwriting.

4. In House Computerized I-card System: Card Master Software is purchased for library to print I - Card. Library has also purchased Haiti I card Printer which enable library to issue PVC I-Card to the students. PVC I-Card has longer life compare to laminated I-Card.

5. Computer Aided Stock Taking : Stock taking of the reading material in the library is a very common practice of quality management to ensure proper functioning of the library and it is also mandatory. The library has to close for stock taking and the manual method of stock taking is very time consuming. As all the libraries are facing the problem of acute shortage of manpower, the readers were unhappy if the library is closed for long time. As the final examination of students get over in the month of May every year and the colleges reopen in the month of June , the librarians get very less time for stock taking work in the library. In such a critical situation computer aided stock taking is really considered a boon. Ness Wadia College library has purchased a DCU (Data Collection Unit). This DCU has facility to read and store barcode, and this barcode can be uploaded in excel file. With the help of this DCU one can do the stock taking work very speedily and accurately.

6. Google Alert Service : Library has created a group of faculty members according to their subject as well as alerts of respective subjects on Google account and sends them regularly.

7. E-alert of New Arrivals : Library has created a group of faculty members on Gmail and list of new arrivals is circulated to them regularly.

3.2.2. Best Practice of Marketing of Library Services:

1. Book Talk : Ness Wadia College of commerce library is arranging book talk called book lovers' group since last 40 years and hundred discussions since 1973 has been arranged. Book lovers group arranging discussions on books in three different languages Marathi, Hindi, English. It consists of a review of books through discussion among the students and presided over by the author of the book himself or well known authority on the topic of the book.

2. Read A Book And Get A Pen : from the year 2012 -2013 library has started a unique activity to motivate students to read more books and inculcating the reading habits among the students. This scheme is applicable to every student XI th Commerce, First year B.Com, BBA, BBM, BCA, students. Library is issuing books to the students and asks to submit a one page abstract of book read, and as a motivation Library is give a pen to the students. Students can get as many as pen they want.

3. Book Review Competition : In Association with the Marathi Department a book review competition for books and Diwali Special Issue (Diwali Ank) is started for First Year students. Students who write best review on books and Diwali Special Issue is felicitated and their review is published in college magazine (Miscellany).

4. Best Reader Prize : To attract and motivate students to read more library books, best reader prize is constituted to the students who read maximum books for the academic year.

5. Exhibition On Special Occasion : On the birth anniversary of our national leaders like Mahatma Gandhi (2nd October), Dr. B.R. Ambedkar (1th April), Swami

Vivekananda (12th January), Savitribai Phule (3rd January) etc. an exhibition of books on these personalities is displayed.

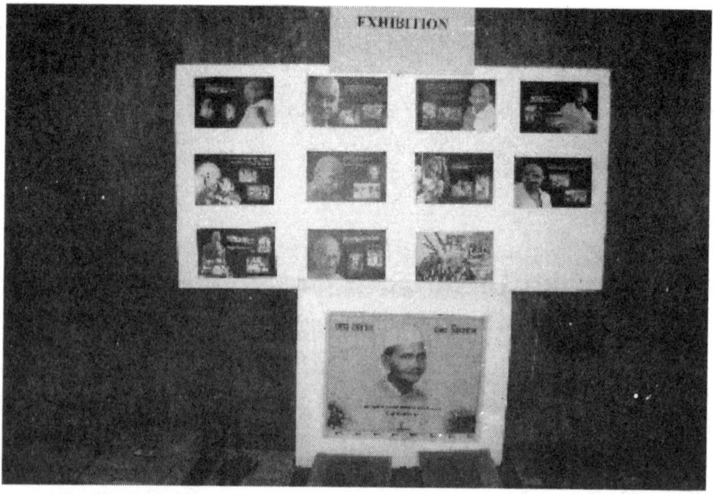

6. Exhibition of New Arrivals : Although the new arrivals display in racks, prior to this an exhibition of new arrivals is arranged for three days where students and staff are allowed to freely browse these books.

7. Exhibition On Different Occasions: Such as authors were felicitated or any award is declared for books or any author passed away, on this occasion books related to them were displayed.

8. Special Collection : A special collection of scared books (Vedas, Ramayana, and Bhagavad-Gita etc) and works of national leaders such as Dr. Babasaheb Ambedkar, Mahatma Gandhi, Pandit Jawaharlal Nehru, and Swami Vivekananda is kept for ready reference and in addition to that separate collection such as personality development, Research Methodology, Biographies of Industrialist, and books for competitive examination are kept for the readers.

9. Library Activities Calendar : Before the starting of academic year, a calendar of library activity is prepared, it helps library to plan and run the activities smoothly. E.g. 3rd January Savitribai Phule birth Anniversary is celebrated by garlanding photo and exhibit books on Savitribai Phule.

10. Literature Quiz : To inculcate the reading habits among the students and motivate them to read good books in the Internet Era, and aware them current as well as classic literature, literature quiz was started by the library. The literature quiz contains questions on World Classic Literature, Hindi, Marathi, English and Sanskrit literature. The winners of the quiz are felicitated with cash prize and certificate of merit.

11. Vacation Reading : Library issues general books in Diwali and summer vacation to the students without any charges and formalities.

12. Utility Counter : A utility counter where stapler, gum, pins, pen is kept handy so users can avail the same. This practice is followed by the college library.

13. Free Distribution Counter : Ness Wadia college library sale discarded books at very low price to the students.

3.2.3. Human Resource Best Practices

1. Birthday Celebration Of Library Employee : To build team spirit among the staff Birth Date of all the library staff is collected and their birthday is celebrated. If any staff member birthday fall on Sunday or holiday their birthday celebrate on next day.

2. Felicitations Of Retired Library Employee : To honor the services of retiring members of staff they are felicitated.

3. Library Services To Retired Staff Members : To keep the association with retired members of the staff their membership to the library is continue as it is.

4. CONCLUSION

It is concluded that best practice are the result and solution of the problems faced by the libraries. All the best practices cannot be adopted blindly but few practices can be adopted after careful study. To meet the users demands effectively the libraries need to study the user's requirement and introduce the best practices, which will be ultimately enhance the goodwill of the library and building moral of the library staff. The success of any best practice is depend upon the financial support from higher authority and whole hearted co-operation of library staff.

10

Best Practices of Dr. T.K.Tope Arts & Commerce Night Senior College, Parel, Mumbai

Nandu Sahebrao More

Librarian, Dr.T.K.Tope Arts & Commerce Night Senior College, Parel, Mumbai.

ABSTRACT

The Purpose of this article is to describe the best practices adopted in Dr.T.K.Tope Arts & Commerce Senior Night College Library such as home lending, Open Access, Free Internet facility, Orientation , best reader award ... etc. These practices are very helpful to the students & staff members.

Keywords : Best Practices, Library Management, Library Orientation

1. INTRODUCTION

The global changes particularly the Information and Communication Technologies (ICT) have impact on the functioning of academic libraries. The developments in ICT have changed the users' expectation from the academic libraries in different ways. The ways to build collection and services to the end users vary from the recent past practices. To meet the end-users demands effectively, the academic libraries need to identify and adopt good practices and benchmarks. Thus, preparing guidelines in a standardized way based on the best practices employed by libraries is significant which will ultimately enhance the value based services of academic libraries.

A method or technique that has consistently shown results superior to those achieved with other means, and that is used as a benchmark. See also best in class and leading practice

1.1. Definitions of Best Practices

Definition of Best Practices **ODLIS** (Online Dictionary of Library and Information Science) describes best practices as follows: "In the application of theory to real-life situations, procedures that, when properly, applied consistently yield superior results and are therefore used as reference points in evaluation of the effectiveness of alternative methods of accomplishing the same task. Best practices are identified by examining empirical evidence of success."

Oxford Advanced Learners Dictionary describes 'best practices as quality of high standard, excellence, highly improved, outstanding, par excellence service. It means way of doing something that is usual or expected way in a particular organization or situation, guidelines for good practices. In this process of developing best practices we take action rather than good ideas, and we improve our skills.'

What is quality? It is customer satisfaction through product or service. In an academic library student and teachers are the customers who are part of the academic community.

2. BEST PRACTICES ADOPTED IN DR.T.K.TOPE ARTS & COMMERCE SENIOR NIGHT COLLEGE LIBRARY

History of the College

Parel is well known as Mumbai's labour area. A large number of young men and women from this area, who were employed, felt the strong desire of the need to obtain a University Degree, either for the sake of better employment or promotion or social awareness. Unfortunately, they did not have the requisite local educational facilities to do so. Again, due to being employed, these young people have only the late evening hours to spare for their studies. It was for these reasons, that the need for a Degree Night College at Parel was felt, and hence established in 1984.

From June 1984, the Government of Maharashtra and the University of Mumbai granted the Gokhale Education Society the permission to start a Night Degree College in Parel from June of that year. Today, the College has become Mumbai's first full-fledged Degree Night Senior College with strength of more than 1000 students. The main objective of the College is to offer academic and co-curricular facilities preferably to employed students.

The Five Laws of Library Science are "Books are for

Use, Every Reader his / her book, Every Book its reader, save the time of reader & The Library is a growing organism". In order to make use of these laws more effective, we are providing following best practices in our library

2.1. Home Lending

Home lending facility is available for the students. At a time two books including one Text book & other on any subjects issued for 7 days can be availed by the students. This intends to inculcate a good reading habit among the students.

2.2. University Book Bank Scheme

This scheme aims at issuing a set of Text books to the reserved category (SC/ST/NT) students. With this availability of books, they can do their reading without ease of borrowing from the library time to time.

2.3. New Arrivals Display

A book-case is prepared to display the newly arrivals so that students and staff will get information and will develop an interest in getting the book issued from the library.

2.4. Book Exhibition

Book Exhibition is organized for the students of Arts & Commerce every year so that they will develop interest in reading books on various subjects available in the library. With this exhibition, a feedback from the staff and students is received to collection issue on concerned subjects.

2.5. Orientation

Orientation programme for FY students is organized to instruct them how to use library, how to get books issued and other sources including internet facility in the library.

2.6. Free Internet Access

Free Internet Access for all students is available in the reading room of the library. With this students can connect themselves to the world of knowledge and at the same time can develop the skill of using Electronic mode of communication.

2.7. Best Reader award

Best Reader Award is conferred on male and female students separately for each academic session. This activity motivates the readers and attracts them for spending their time in reading

2.8. Availability of Reading room on holidays

A month before and during the exam time, reading room is made available on all holidays for the students.

2.9. Guest Talk on Information Sources

Guest Lecture on "Gateway to Knowledge" was organized on 12th September 2014. This helped the students to know about various resources available for getting information on various subjects.

2.10. Notice Board

Library has separate notice board on which various circulars and notices displayed for students and staff.

2.11. Information of Library in Prospects

College prospect includes the required details of the library informing the students about library hours, library card and other services.

2.12. Previous Years Question Paper Sets

Old question papers of all subjects are issued from the library for the students so that they can make the preparation for the examination.

2.13. Open Access

Open access facility is availed by the students. With this choice they can refer the resources of their interest.

2.14. Library Automation Software

SOUL 2.0 Library software for automation has been installed in the library.

5. CONCLUSION

The role of library among higher education is indisputable. The Dr.T.K.Tope College Library is no exception for the same. This College library has adopted many best practices as a routine task of library activity. By adoption of the best practices there will be continuous improvement and performance. The best practices adopted should bridge the gap between library and users for maximum utilization of the resources.

REFERENCES

1. www.oxfordlearnersdictionaries.com/
2. www.library.ucsb.edu
3. Library and Information Science: A Case Presentations retrieved from www.naac.gov
4. www. http://tktopenightcollege.in/

11

Best Practices at Maeer's Mitsom Library

Nitin S Joshi

Librarian, MAEER's MIT School of Management, Pune

ABSTRACT

Adoptions of library science rule Padamshree Dr. S.R. Ranganathan in each activity in the libraries of any types of library will be the best practices. A best practice may be innovative and be a philosophy, policy, strategy, program, process or practice that solves a problem or create new opportunities and positively impact the whole organization. If one thinks with an open and creative mind, in almost every aspect of library a range of best practices can be evolved. Best practices are nothing but developing tailor made services, reaching beyond with available resources and delighting the users. The paper discussed the challenges faced by the college libraries and best practices adopted in MITSOM library.

Keywords : Best Practices, Library Services, Academic libraries, Library Administration, Management. MITSOM etc.

1. INTRODUCTION

Academic libraries mostly support learning, teaching and research process in the institutes. Collection and library decorum are indispensable assets of any library especially in an academic library. These aspects develops image of the library. Almost all the services and outputs of a library are associated with these two aspects. These can be strengthened further with the help of additional best practices. The role and challenges faced with the adoption of the best practices in academic libraries there will be a continuous improvement and overall performance in the institution. The college library acts as vehicle for disseminating the information and the related ICT through the best practices for utilization by its user's community and also for the exchange of information among its users.

2. DEFINITION

Methods and techniques that have consistently shown result superior to those achieved with other means and which are used as benchmarks to strive for. There is however no practice that is best for everyone or in every situation and no best practice remain best for very along as people keep on finding better ways of doing things.

ODLIS (Online Dictionary of Library and Information Science)

"In the application of theory to real-life situations, procedures that, when properly applied, consistently yield superior results and are therefore used as reference points in evaluation the effectiveness of alternative methods of accomplishing the same task".

3. ROLE OF THE ACADEMIC LIBRARIES

The role of the library in a college is aimed at realizing the educational goals of the college or the parent Organization. The college libraries not only provides motivation to reading by procuring materials for study And research, by introducing open access system, by providing long hours of open, by organizing the library Resources in a systematic way, but also feed the intellect of the student, encourage the researches of the Faculty and thus serve the teaching and research needs of the faculty, The college library acts as a vehicle for

Disseminating information and the related ICT through the best practices for utilization by its user's community and also for the exchange of information among its users.

4. IMPLEMENTATION OF BEST PRACTICES

To implement best practices in the library in a systematic way is important to get the maximum results. It Can be achieved by following four stages,

Identification : Identification of the weaknesses of the library service areas and best practices accordingly Important thing is that library in charge has to identify the need of the users and accordingly set some Practice so that the users can get maximum benefit.

Implementation : Strategy for implementation is to be decided.

Dissemination : Users should be informed about the services rendered by the library. Proper dissemination is needed.

Utilization-User feedback : Frequent feedback of the users is important to improvement the facilities.

The Best Practices are classified under the following broad areas

1. Management and administration of a library
2. Collection and Services
3. Extent of use of services
4. Use of technology in libraries

4. CHALLENGES FACED BY ACADEMIC LIBRARIES

a) Explosive growth of information and documents

b) Increased cost of the documents and information materials

c) Increase in users information needs

d) New role of librarian and greater responsibilities.

e) Latest techniques and concepts in handing of information

f) New electronic information environment

g) Creation of database and its security

h) Marketing of library and information services.

4. BEST PRACTICES IN MAEER'S MITSOM LIBRARY

Following best practices are adopted in MAEER's MITSOM Library.

1. Practice :

Locker system for users

Goal of the practice

1. User belonging should be safe and his/her own responsibility

The process:

1. User can choose his/her locker. Total 90 Ninety Lockers available
2. Lock and key is available for each locker, student can get his/her key from circulation counter and give his/her I-card.
3. Users can use locker for one day only
4. If he is not return key same day fine of Rs. 10 will charged.

Impact of the practice:

1. Till date no compliant form users
2. Without peon or person the system is functions well

2. Practice

User Automated entry register

Goal of the practice

1. Library Statistics - walk in library

The process

1. Every user scan I-card at entrance
2. Data can take at excel file or SLIM 21 software also.

Impact of the practice

1. Addition in library automation
2. Statistics can be used at any time for various reports- LIC, DTE, AICTE, NAAC, NBA etc.

3. Practice

HBS Corner

Goal of the practice

HBS-Harvard Business School Publication at one place

The process

As an when new book will be added to section

Impact of the practice

Researcher and facility members find it's very useful. It is appreciate by outsiders and specially the committee members

4. Practice

Reference section –Act/Handbooks/Volumes/ Dictionaries etc.....

Goal of the practice

Highlight the collection for increase the usages.

The process

New addition to collection directly goes to classified section

Impact of the practice

Classified collection easily come to know for users

Easily located, Usage is Increase; It will add value to collection as well as image of library.

5. Practice

General books- a-z classification

Goal of the practice

Attraction for users and useful/increase reading habits.

The process

General book will kept as per Title – ABCD.....XYZ

Impact of the practice

It will easily find the title

Usages increase

Popular amongst students

6. Practice

Compliments book for students

Goal of the practice

Efforts towards Personality development of students

The process

Every new student will get 3 books

Impact of the practice

Students ask for more title

It will value addition to library

Well appreciated by outsiders, committee members

7. Practice

Best library users award for students & Faculty members

Goal of the practice

Increase the library usages for academic as well as general

The process

Awardees will choose from the statistics for academic and general usages of resources

Impact of the practice

Hadley completion amongst the users

It will help for collection development

8. Practice

Library at a Glance/ statistics

Goal of the practice

Avoid misunderstanding/wrong information amongst users, staff and management and specially the various committee members

The process

Update information every month and specially the visits of various committees.

Impact of the practice

Everybody comes to know the library at a glance

Without fear and confidentially handled committee authorities.

10. Practice

9) Library copy

Goal of the practice

Text book one copy available for ready reference within library

To avoid unconvinced of the users.

The process

As a when new text book added in library one copy will kept aside.

Impact of the practice

It will avoid unconvinced of users.

Very useful when all text books issued

10. Practice

Biographies /autobiography section

Goal of the practice

Motivate the students and enrich library collection

Impact of the practice

Value addition to library collection

Students eagerly waiting for new addition

11. Practice

Index alert through institute website -www.mitsom.org

Goal of the practice

Increase usages of Journals & Periodicals

The process

Monthly updated the Index of subject related journals and periodicals

Impact of the practice

It will add value to library services

Very well appreciated by users within campus and outsiders

12. Practice

Library week celebration – Organizing Exhibition/ workshop/seminar etc.

Goal of the practice

Increase network amongst professionals and sharing the expertise, professional development.

Impact of the practice

Good number of suggestion received for betterment of library Network increased day by day

13. Practice

Library orientation

Goal of the practice

Everything know out library

The process

Every year new student's orientation within class room and visit to library- using PPT.

Impact of the practice

Librarian knows personally by students and faculty members.

Relation development

15. Practice

Student Personal book purchase

Goal of the practice

Institutional discount will benefit to students personal book purchase.

The process

Impact of the practice

Students walk in library increase

Increase CRM – Customer Relation Management.

16. Practice

NOC- No Objection Certificate Feedback systems

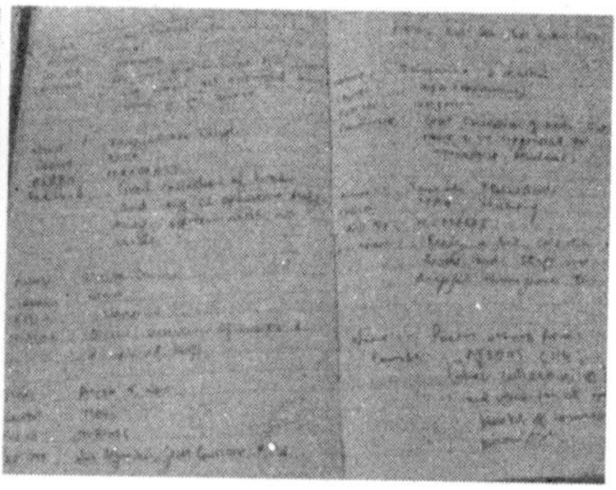

Goal of the practice

Know the image/opinion of overall library from student's users.

The process

When students came for NOC we take free-open feedback from each student,

He/she has to give open feedback about overall library.

Impact of the practice

It will add to library overall development

Most of practices came from user's feedback

17. Practice

ITC USE

a) Automated stock verification through Wireless Data collector.

Bar Code Technology adapted for circulation.

Q-papers & Syllabus available through LAN.

Goal of the practice

Using ITC in library will value addition to library and minimize the error and increase the accuracy in library process.

Impact of the practice

It will save the time cost and energy

Stock verification was easily done about disturbing library operations.

CONCLUSION

About the Best Practices we can learn and improve a lot from the excellent other institutes that adopted best practices. The Best Practices is an attitude, an approach or a philosophy based on the desire for continuous learning and improvement. Improve our quality in changing environment we should adopt more and more good practices. We can Identify and adopt the best practices of the college library. The best practices are evolved through stages of failures and correction and through the borrowed best practices we can enhance our competitive advantage and also enhance the institutional effectiveness. Best Practices requires active participation, willingness, creativity and problem solving attitude from the library stakeholders. Best Practices do not have one template or everyone to follow.

REFERENCES

1 Gokhale, K. (2013) Best Practices in Academic Libraries: Case of MAEER's MIT Library. SALIS Journal of Library and Information Sciecne. 5(1), 73-79.

2. Umesh, K.Y (2012) Best practices adopted in academic libraries and information resource centers. International Journal of Information Dissemination and Technology, 2(3), 186-188

3 Tikam. M.V (2010) Best practices in Academic Libraries (http://liscompendium)

4 Kulkarni S. A (2009) Best practices in libraries. Library and Information Services in changing Era (Proceeding of the National Seminar, University of Pune) Pune January 22-33, 2009. Pp.273-280.

5 NAAC: Best practices in library and information services (*www.naac.gov.in.*) Library and information services: case presentations. NAAC, 2006

12

Best Practices of Gandhi Shikshan Bhavan's, Smt. Surajaba College of Education

Pradnya Anil Bhosekar
Librarian, Gandhi Shikshan Bhavan's,
Smt. Surajaba College of Education,
Juhu Road (north), Juhu Mumbai 400049.

ABSTRACT

Gandhi Shikshan Bhsvan's Surajaba College of Education. Vision of the college is to develop involved,dedicated,innovative and socially committed and active teachers. Library provides services accordingly.

BEST PRACTICES OF OUR LIBRARY

1. Bookbank service
2. Book exhibitions
3. Book Exhibitions For school children
4. Granth vruksha

Gandhi Shikshan Bhavan's Smt Surajaba College of Education is established in June 1970. It is located in Juhu area of Mumbai. Our college's moto is 'Learning to teach and teaching to learn'. College works for development of well integrated personality. Our vision is development of involved, dedicated innovative and socially committed and active teachers. The library follows thesame vision.

Some of the best practices of our library

1. Bookbank facility : Library provides 4 books to each students per semester. Priority is given to poor students. Mainly textbooks of the subjects are provided in this bookbank facility. As per feedbackof the students', this is very useful to them.

2. Exhibition : Theme based exhibitions are arranged frequently in the library. Eg. Books on women, books on Tagorian literature, books on Gandhian literature, books based on early child education etc. to name a few.

3. Book exhibition for school children : For inculcating reading habits among school children, library organizes display of small story books, pictorial books etc. Students visit this exhibition with their teachers and enjoy reading.

4. Granth Vruksha : Books that are normally not in demand but very important, old but useful to the students are displayed once in a week. Normally library changes this book on every Monday.

Eg. A cosmic adventure by Jayant Narlikar, Guide to places of the world, Know India better etc.

5. Creation of teaching aids : As part of curriculum students have to givelessons in the schools.Librarian, with the help of faculty members, creates teaching aids that help students conduct different lessons. Preservation and dissemination of teaching aids are done by library.

6. At the entrance of the library, space is provided for display. Library displays different charts on various themes on the display board which includes pictures, quotations, information etc. These charts are made by librarian with the help of faculty members.

7. Question papers and grey literature is available in digitised form. Students can get this online facility.

8. Free internet serviceas well as photocopying facility is available in library.

9. Librarian conducts book review programme. She orients students, issues books for book review and her plan is to compile these reviews at end of the year.

10. Library provides unrestricted books to the students and staff.

11. As ours is Gandhian institute library provides one book written by Gandhiji to each student and ask to write 5 stories whichever they like.

CONCLUSION

In the process of achieving best practices in libraries, Prof. A.C. Tikekar warns us "Blind imitation, false competition and status symbolism do not work well. Adhocism too does not accomplish the desired goal.Ill planned radical change would prove costly and unwieldy. At the same time both resistance and reluctance to accept the inevitable changes will be harmful to development of libraries." Keeping this in mind librarian should achieve best practices in library.

13

Best Practices in Library of Nirmala Niketan College of Home Science, Mumbai

Prajakata P. Mhaprolkar
Librarian, Nirmala Niketan college of Home Science,
49, New Marine Lines, Mumbai

ABSTRACT

The University Grand Commission and higher education are concerned about the quality of higher education and they want to develop higher education infrastructure keeping in view the quality as standard. Libraries are an important part of higher education. Libraries tries to provide maximum service for students, staff and outsider readers in minimum cost. The role of NAAC in college library development is very important to develop library through the library best practices. In this paper I have stated the current status and the best practices of the library of Nirmala Niketan college of Home Science.

Keywords : Higher Education, NAAC, University Grand Commission, Library

INTRODUCTION

Globalization is playing a major role in making today's students more focused and demanding. At the same time Information and Communication Technologies

(ICT) have changed the users' expectation from the academic libraries in different ways. The demand of the users varies from the past to recent practices. So the huge number of academic institutions in India it needs efforts to bring quality in library services immediately.

Library and Information Services of Higher Education institutions play a central role in enhancing the quality of academic and research environment. It is because of this reason Government of India, UGC and NAAC are seriously concerned about how to improve standards of education and Introduce best practices in the universities and colleges and their libraries. The services of the libraries has been expanding as they contribute significantly to the learning process, particularly the e-learning process

In this scenario, only those libraries can excel and satisfy its users which can develop best practices with the available resources.

MEANING OF BEST PRACTICES IN LIBRARIES

A best practice may be innovative and be a philosophy, policy, strategy, program, process or practice that solves a problem or create new opportunities and positively impact the whole organization (NAAC, 2006). If one thinks with an open and creative mind, in almost every aspect of library a range of best practices can be evolved. Collection and library environment are indispensable assets of any library, especially in an academic library.

Concise Oxford English Dictionary describes 'Best practices as quality of most excellent or desirable type or most appropriate, advantageous, highly improved, outstanding, par excellence services or the customary or expected procedure or way of doing something that is usual or expected way in a particular organization or situation, guidelines for good practices. In this process of developing best practices, we take action rather than good ideas, and we improve our skills.'

NATIONAL ASSESSMENT AND ACCREDITATION COUNCIL (NAAC)

National Assessment and Accreditation Council (*NAAC*) were established by the UGC in September 1994 in Bangalore for evaluating the performance of the Universities and Colleges in the Country. NAAC's mandate includes the task of performance evaluation, assessment and accreditation of universities and colleges in the country. The philosophy of NAAC is based on objective and continuous improvement rather than being punitive or judgmental, so that all institutions of higher learning are empowered to maximize their resources, opportunities and capabilities. Assessment is a performance evaluation of an institution and /or its units and is accomplished through a process based on self-study and peer review using defined criteria. Accreditation refers to the certification given by NAAC, which is valid for a period of five years. At present the Assessment and Accreditation by NAAC is done on a voluntary basis.

NAAC strives for Quality and excellence in higher education and advocates for enhancing the role of library and Information Services in improving academic environment. A document prepared by NAAC for Best Practices in Academic Libraries says "Best Practices may be innovative and be a philosophy, policy, and Strategy program, Processor Practice that solves a problem or create new opportunities and positive impact on organizations." NAAC developed a set of Best Practices followed in academic Libraries and presented under the following four broad areas:

A) Management and Administration of Library

B) Collection and Services

C) Extent of user Services

D) Use of Technology

NIRMALA NIKETAN COLLEGE LIBRARY (NAAC-A GRADE)

The Library of COLLEGE OF HOME SCIENCE AND POLYTECHNIC, NIRMALA NIKETAN, Mumbai-20 established in 1955, the same year when the college came into being. The library is located on the fourth floor of the main building of the college. Mrs. Urmila R. Shah. Served as the first librarian of the college library from 1955.

College library is the gateway to knowledge, provides a basic condition for lifelong learning, independent decision-making, and cultural development of the students and the teachers. Focusing upon the very important role of the library, our college Library has been growing steadily over the years.

RENOVATION

The library has been renovated in the year 2010-2011 considering the space limitations and the ever-increasing demand for new books & reading materials. Storage had been a perennial problem, hence the renovation project was taken up. The layout of book racks has been planned to increase the natural illumination levels during day. This arrangement has also added to the illusion of depth, making the space look bigger. The colour scheme chosen, off-whites & natural browns have further enhanced the aesthetics of the place. Six cameras have been installed in prominent locations inside the library to tackle the theft of books & tearing of pages from the reference books. The librarian is now able to monitor every corner of the library with ease & efficiency.

(A) Management and Administration of Library

Listed below are the best practices adopted by the NN Library in the management and administration of the library system. An effective management of library supports excellence in the students, supports divergent research needs on and off campus, continues to adopt changes, and contributes in strengthening the academic life on the campus of the college.

LIBRARY MAINTENANCE

The library is a place where many users visit to read, consult and borrow reading materials. Inviting, clean and tidy atmosphere is necessary in and outside the Library. Maintain decorum of the library is very much required to concentrate reading and searching of materials.

Nirmala Niketan Library has concentrated to achieve this to provide the users clean and green environment, including dust free environment in the stack and reading areas. Nirmala Niketan library support staff maintained cleanliness in/outside the library punctually on regular basis. Library Users appreciate and cooperate the library efforts in keeping the entrance, reading and stack areas neat and clean.

TRAINING PROGRAM

Department of Life Long Learning and Extension offers an extension programme under which various projects have been arranged for students. Aim if this project is to sensitize the students to the socio - cultured realities and improve their personality.

The projects are career oriented as well as community oriented. Our college department of Community Resources Management has taken up the Industrial Orientation project for the students. 2 Students were placed in our college Library under the supervision of librarian to perform a library work. They are helping to library staff for maintaining shelf order of stock, shelving of the collection as per classification scheme, processing of forwarding & recommendations receiving from users, acquisition process as well as the maintenance of various library sections.

LIBRARY COMMITTEE

There is a library advisory committee, which includes the principal, the librarian, the accountant, and senior faculty members from each of the specializations (e.g., FND, HD, TFT, and CRM).

The committee meets at least twice a year; moreover, the principal meets the librarian, the accountant, heads of specialization, and library committee staff members separately for urgent ad hoc library matters.

Policy initiatives of the committee for increasing library usage: Annual awards/recognition for students who have issued the maximum number of books. Other policy initiatives of the library committee: Annual book exhibition in college.

B. COLLECTION AND SERVICES

Listed below are the best practices followed in selected libraries in the area of collection and information services

ECC Lab Material

The ECCE Lab material stored in the library, is meant for the use of the TYBSc (HD) students for the DAP practical as well as for the MSc 1 (HD) students for their ECCE practical.

The material consists of Developmentally Appropriate puppets, soft toys, flashcards, games and toys to use as teaching aids. Some of the material was especially purchased for the ECCE Lab, while some of it has been developed by the students during their practicals over the years. This material has also been put to good use during the Department Mela activity for street children over the years.

Weeded out of old and tattered books

In the Library there is no space for new books so the library committee decided to weed out old books. The library should display all old and tattered books, according to the department and Teachers should take the decision for the same . Library Committee makes policies to weed out old books to accommodate new and latest edition.

Stock taking of Library Collection

Every year stock taking is conducted. Missing books/periodicals/video tapes/CDs are listed according to their accession number and those documents are kept in the search for three years. If still those books are not found, then the list of them with their costs is forwarded to the management to write them off from the record of the library.

If a reader loses a book, he is asked to replace the copy. If the book is not available in the market, then the cost of the book is recovered from the reader and the book is written off from the record of the library.

Book Exhibition

To have a glance at recent publications and to facilitate bulky purchase of books, the College library hold two days book Exhibition in the library. Our students and staff members have selected a good book for libraries and their personal reading.

Reference Service

The staff of the library and librarian help the readers in finding their queries. Readers are also provided with relevant documents, which are of interest to them and they are shown the technique of finding information.

Bibliographic Service

List of books is provided to the faculty as well as students if it is demanded by them. Also the list of the new arrival is given to respective departments.

Artical Indexing

The library is providing Indexing of articles from

the research journals facility to the library users. It's very useful for PhD and M. Sc students for their research work.

Card Catalogue

Card catalogue (Author, Title and Subject) have been provided to have an easy access to the collection of the library. Also the readers are helped in browsing the OPAC and the card catalogue.

Inter Library Loan Facility

The College Library provides inter library loan facility to its readers to cater to the extra reading needs of its readers.

Following are the institutions, which are interconnected with our college library.

1. Nirmala Niketan College of Social Work, Mumbai
2. SNDT University, Mumbai
3. Anjuman Anjuman -I- Islam's A.K. Hafizka Institute of Hotel Management & Catering Technology

Display of New Arrivals

New books, which are recently added to the library collection, are displayed in the glassed display racks. So that students and faculty will come to know about them.

C. EXTENT OF THE USE OF SERVICES

Besides the traditional user education and feedback of the users, there are a few user education and use measurement practices which are essential for academic libraries. Some of the best practices followed in measuring and enhancing the use of the services of NN Library are outlined below:

Library Orientation

The library orientation is conducted every year for newcomers in the college. The library staff takes the students to the library and introduces them with OPAC facility, arrangement of the collection of books and other Library materials and services offered to them. Also, they are made aware of the rules and regulations of the library. During orientation, we distribute the Library brochure to the students.

Best Reader's Award

The Library Committee has instituted a 'BEST READER OF THE YEAR AWARD' to be given to the students from this year i.e. 2009-10. The criteria would be as mentioned below.

i. Regular use of books, especially Reference Books,
ii. Active interest in keeping touch with the periodicals,
iii. Proper use of Audio Visual facility,
iv. Observation of library norms and discipline.

The Library Committee will invite applications from Degree College students and interview the aspirants. Two students will be selected. The award will be in the form of a certificate and a rotating trophy.

Book Review Compition

The Library of NirmalaNikitan Collage of home science is conducting a book Review competition for junior college student.

The criteria for judging this competition will be:

Feedback of any book read... Fiction/non Fiction; which includes:

- How well the book has achieved its goal
- What possibilities are suggested by the book
- What the book has left out
- How the book compares to others on the subject
- What specific points are not convincing
- What personal experience have you had related to the subject

Grievance Redressal mechanism of the Library

1. Consultation with a Librarian : Students can consult with the librarian any problems related to the library and its services. The librarian tries to solve them in his/her capacity otherwise or forward them to the Principal of the college.

2. Suggestion Box : A suggestion box is kept in the library seeking valuable suggestions and recommendations from the readers of the library. The suggestions made by them are taken up and D Use of Information Technology in Libraries discussed in the library committee meeting and healthy suggestions are implemented.

D. USE OF INFORMATION TECHNOLOGY IN LIBRARIES

Library Services need to reach to the user desktops with the use of Information Technology (IT). It uses technology in library with specific goals and objectives.These are some practical examples for the NN library, wish to adopt in library with suitable modification based on requirements.

Web OPAC (Online Public Access Catalogue)

In 2009, Nirmala Niketan library purchased new software, SLIM 21 to make the library retrieval tool WEBOPAC on the Web for wider access. Library collection availability and its status are very important for the users.On this WEBOPAC attached various useful data.

Internet Facility

IT Zone with 10 computers for staff or student use (2 of these are used by library staff), all are with Internet facility. Internet bandwidth/ speed "2 mbps VPN broadband connection is available in the library.

The staff uses the Internet free of charge. Students are charged a nominal rate. Library e-resources are available through these computers.

Audio and Video Cassettes and CDs

The library has a collection of 82 audio, 144videocassettes and 351 CDs on varying subjects. Readers can borrow them for current use only.

E-Journals

The College library has subscribed 9 e -journals for library which are using by the PhD and M. Sc students.

Wi-Fi

From September 2014 Library are given the facility of Wi-Fi for students of the library for their project work and preparing seminar presentations.

Other Computerized Activites of the Library (Library Automation)

In 2009 the library purchased new software, SLIM 21. The cost of the software is 1,55000/-

- Lending of the books (Issue and Return to staff and Students)
- Acquisition of Books/CDs /Bound volumes / dissertation
- Library Database
- E- Journals
- Acquisition of Bound Volumes
- Bar Coding of Books with a barcode scanner
- Bibliography (list of Books/Dissertation /Journals /Bound Volumes)
- Library Website: Library email id; university library website
- Electronic Resource Management package for e-journals: Inflibnet N-List Program

CONCLUSION

In this paper researcher confined that as per NAAC guidelines Nirmala Niketan library adopted various best practices in its administration, management, collection & services, Extent of the Use of Services and use of technology. NN Library implemented the Information literacy and user awareness programs with normative practices through best practices. In its effective implementation that make significant change in enhancing the use of information sources/services and user satisfaction level.

REFERENCES

1. NAAC. (2006) *Best Practices in Library and Information Services.* [online] Available from: http://www.naac.gov.in/best_practices (Accessed on dt.12/02/2015)
2. NAAC. (2006) *Library and Information Services: A Case Presentations.* [online] Available from: http://www.naac.gov.in/casepresentations (Accessed on dt.12/02/2015)
3. *<http://www.abc-clio.com/ODLIS/searchODLIS.aspx>* (Accessed on dt. 20/02/2015)
4. *<https://en.wikipedia.org/wiki/Best_practice>* (Acessed on dt.3/2/2015)
5. Nirmla Niketan College Magazine (year 2009 -2014)
6. *<http://nirmalaniketan.com/naac-rar-submission/pdf/ssr-2009-2014.pdf(Accessed>* on dt. 19and 20/02.2015)

14

Generating "Best Practices" to Galvanize the Quality in Academic Libraries

Pratibha.A. Kanojia
Librarian, Secondary Training College,
3, Mahapalika Marg, Dhobi Talao, Mumbai-400001.

ABSTRACT

Quality Indicator are very useful and pathway to transfer library role traditional to Modern and well maintain library. Library will get special effort in future to membership of national and international institution database for use of index, e-journal, e-books and other service. Naturally the institutional quality bench marking is started to achieve the next quality milestone. As a result the institutes are supposed to identify, generate and monitor the best practices to galvanize their quality. Library should maintain quality through all above practice mentioned in this paper. All data are also enrolled in various register and SOUL report from day to day work.

Key Words : Historical Aspect, concept of best practice Need for the best practices,

INTRODUCTION

Globalization era, giving commercial approach to higher education has naturally brought in the concept of "Best practice". With this point of view the NAAC has after wide consultation evolved a set of guidelines on quality indicators, to help academic libraries to be always in their best form. The of quality management system and techniques in libraries can increasing productivity while focusing on the customer's needs. College libraries are required to study space need while allocating the seating space, good collection, technical work, use of modern technology by user and staff, to meet the modern challenges. The Libraries need to prepare well framed rules and guidelines with regards to hours of access, circulation policies, and other regulations to offer better services to the user.

However from the initiation of the NAAC in 1994, "Best practice" is the most discussed but least practiced term in the process of quality enhancement of the Indian higher education institutes. The institutes least academic in their approach and reporting irrelevant things for their best practices is an irony of quality education. "Best Practice", an essential key aspect of every criterion of the previous assessment manual of the NAAC has been placed separately in the seventh criterion of the recently improved manual in 2012. Through this article the researcher intends to discuss the concept of the "Best Practices".

Libraries are including in IV criteria of the NAAC Accreditation Standards, Which is prepared for data collection.

HISTORICAL ASPECT

NAAC does the assessment of a library vital subunit, is a key step that integrates itself with the overall evaluation. Library is the fulcrum of support for the entire range of Academic activities on an Educational campus. In today High-tech learning resource sis taking up increasingly more academic space and time in the life of learner. In time ahead, this will be even more so.All this play up the need for scientific evaluation of the library.

So that its role as the centerpiece of academic development is protected and enhanced. It is in this context that the NAAC has after wide consultations evolved a set of Guidelines on quality indicator, to help academic libraries to be always in their best form.

THE CONCEPT OF BEST PRACTICES

There is a clear cut clarification of the concept of best practice in the SSR (Manual for the self-study report 2012) by the NAAC, that the "Best Practices "are the practice of the Institution leading to improvement and having visible impact. Best practice has come to refer to the most preferred way of performing a certain task or tackling a particular challenge, as opposed to any other way.

In these days Quality works best practice are the quality indicator of the institute. Library play very important in Quality works and presentation. The display the visionary management, the creativity of the leadership, the institutional commitment to quality and its academic vibrancy. Wikipedia defines "Best Practices" as a method that has consistently shown results superior to those achieved with other means and that is used as a benchmark. It is an operating practice or a strategic management term, a proven way of doing something which will not harm but help others. It is followed as a process that is known to produce near-optimum results.

THE NEED FOR THE BEST PRACTICES

The NAAC believes in the intuitional excellence rather than the competition so it is the competition within. Once the concept internalized, it could be easily institutionalized. Practiced in spirit, the Best Practices can give a separate identity to the institute. While proving the relevance of benchmarking of the best practices.

Some of the best practice which can improve the quality of the Library are as follows:

1. Management of Library & Information Services

In a large and very old college Library the environment often defines the use of the library in term of the strength and size of text and research collection. The library supports general information requirements of the users, both study and research. By considering set minimum parameters lists below would help to ensure quality in library systems.

1. Working hours : This parameter refers to opening and closing hours of the library. Timing of library should be flexible for the user so that they can enjoy reading and sit in the library.

2. Library Advisory Committee : This formation of library committee with an equal representation by faculty and students and the role of the committee and its functions in developing library service are to be well defined.

3. Manpower Development : Qualification and experience of the librarian and the library staff should be on par with that of the academic staff and should fulfill the norms prescribed by UGC/NCTE etc. Training programs and professional involvement of library professional need to be encouraged.

4. Infrastructure of the Library : The aspect of location of the library. The library has a place of its own with proper planning and organization of space and has proper furniture, necessary quantity and quality of reading chairs, tables, display racks, magazine racks, etc. area for service counters and other section of the library as prescribed by government and other governing bodies are to be taken note of along with proper ventilation, fan, and water and toilet facilities. Fixing of notice board, Research cubicles for Scholars/Teachers, along with due attention to overall building maintenance and cleanliness also need consideration.

5. ICT Infrastructure and Know-How : Quantification and computer facilities, system for enabling e-library services, etc. Need to be determined, taking in to account total number of user, type of users and programs offered. The library should have networking facility and be a part of institution network, with fully implemented automation. The bandwidth of internet access and subscription, organization and access of e-resources, etc. are important factors in the transmission of digital information services.

6. Overall Policy of the Institution on Library : The library should have an approved policy on collection development support, in term of fund annual increase of budget, binding procedure, removal of obsolete books and policy on loss of books and an ongoing commitment of the institution in deputing library professional for continuing and further education.

7. Budget : There should be a proportionate growth in the library budget for different document in such as book, journals and other resources and ICT infrastructure are to be defined UGC grants are the source of income for enhancing the collection and services.

2. Collection

The library is required to provide varied, and up-to –date resources date resources that support its mission and the needs of its users moreover, resources may be in a variety of formats, including print or hard copy, online electronic text or image and other media. They may be in the form of books, textbooks standard reference, current journals which include national international and peer reviewed journals, back volume ,e-resources, government document, book-bank rare material collection for competitive exams,etc. Even with limited budget the library may explore ways, such as open access sources to provide quality resources.

3. Services

The library has a key role in supporting the academic activities of the institutions by establishing, maintaining and promoting the library and information service.

BEST PRACTICE FOR MY COLLEGE LIBRARY

In the library context, the best practice may be viewed as one. Listed below is suggestive set of best practices.

1. Library Brochure/Dairies
2. Central reference library for the use of constituent and affiliated colleges.
3. A feedback form, questionnaire, should be done at least twice year.
4. Compiling and displaying of student /teacher attendance statistics (graphic) on the notice boards of the library as well as in the departments.
5. Displaying a new arrivals books/journals.
6. Suggestion box and timely response.
7. Development of website /webpage for library including all the services and necessary information.
8. Establishing linkage with other libraries and avail free.
9. Development of electronic environment on the campus
10. Conducting Exhibitions/Demonstrations/Lecture on current Issues.

CONCLUSION

Since education has been proved international service in the globalization era quality is essential "Best Practices" the concept from the industry is a part of the management of higher education today.

NAAC Quality indicators are very useful and

pathway to transfer library role traditional to modern and well maintained library. Library will get special effort in future to membership of national or international institution database for use of index, e-journal, e-books and other service which provided through their database.

Library should maintain quality through all above practices mention in the paper. All statistical data is also enrolled in various register and SOUL report from day to day work. All things of library work is in written from as like rules of library and reading room goal and mission, future work etc., it is a part of Quality maintenance.

After studying Best Practices do the work of Galvanize the quality of college Library?

REFERENCES

1. NAAC Publication (2007) Best Practice
2. En.Wikidpedia.org/wiki/Best practice
3. Pathan, S.N. NAAC A Success story of Maharashtra: 1st ed 2005, Intellectual book bureau, Bhopal.
4. NAAC (2012) Manual for the self - study report Innovations and Best practices Criterion.
5. NAAC : Guidelines on Quality Indicators in library and information service,
6. WWW.naac.india.com.

15

Best Practices in Academic Libraries : A Case Study of Bhurani College of Commerce & Arts, Mazgaon, Mumbai

Sujata Sunil Rajpurkar
Librarian, Burhani College of Commerce & Arts. Mazgaon, Mumbai.

ABSTRACT

Academic Libraries (and librarians) have an opportunity to improve the quality of undergraduate education and to contribute overall development of the young generation. In order to achieve this, academic libraries need to broaden conceptualization of the role of the academic library, beyond collecting, organizing and preserving materials. In other words, the academic library becomes indispensable part of teaching learning process, which is actively involved in all aspects of higher education—teaching, research and community service. In order to achieve objective of maximum utilization of library resources, we at BCCA library (Burhani College of commerce and arts library) undertakes many activities which are student centric, in present paper author discusses the best practices that are conducted to achieve the stated objective.

Keywords : Academic library, library best practices, innovative library practices, Library services.

"To build up a library is to create a life. It's never just a random collection of books."

— Carlos Maria Dorminguez

INTRODUCTION

Academic libraries has very important role to play in nation building. In order to form future of young generation libraries need to acquire, organizing and provide various library resources and library services to the staff and students. Academic Libraries (and librarians) have an opportunity to improve the quality of undergraduate education and to contribute overall development of the young generation. They are strong crusader of belief that preservation and conservation of information and knowledge is important as they are contributing to create a strong, culturally literate, and educated society.

In order to achieve this, academic libraries need to broaden conceptualization of the role of the academic library, beyond collecting, organizing and preserving materials. In other words, the academic library becomes indispensable part of teaching learning process, which is actively involved in all aspects of higher education—teaching, research and community service. A teaching library is characterized by its commitments to instructing students, faculty and staff; to fostering a climate which encourages lifelong learning; to maintaining a collection which stimulates inquiry; to making the library the cultural center for the campus and community; and to engaging in research to improve library services (Allen 2000)

Due to the development in science and technology and information explosion now a days it is possible to provide maximum resources and services which would satisfy the end user needs. Gone are the days when academicians totally depend on the library collection, Information technology like any other fields has strong impact on library and information science too. Students are fascinated towards the Google and smart phones to obtain the required information; in this scenario teaching students to use the library and attract them towards the library is becoming very challenging task for both the librarians and teachers.

In order to achieve objective of maximum utilization of library resources, we at BCCA library (Burhani College of commerce and arts library) to inculcate more reading habits and to boost love for books and knowledge library undertakes many activities which are student centric and are conducted by keeping in mind the academic and professional needs of young generation. These activities help students to explore their inherent skills and also gave them opportunity to express themselves through different sources. Some are described below.

Burhani College of commerce and arts library over the past 43 years has emerged as a very rich library. It is well equipped with a large collection of books, periodicals, journals and audio - visual resources which are required for teaching learning process and for the overall development of its students and the staff.

EXTENDED BOOK DISPLAY

With the co-ordination and co-operation with other departments BCCA library organizes theme based book displays which are connected to different collegiate and intercollegiate competitions. After detail discussion with the faculty members book displays are organized in the library, students are actively contributing in this book displays, faculty members suggesting the theme and titles of the books and the whole responsibility given to the students, students with the help of library staff arranging display with their innovative ideas, they glorified display with their creativity and presenting information of the book in such a way that the nonuser of the library also get attracted towards the library collection and thus this activity increased our circulation volume and readership. The remarkable point of these displays is that Junior college students have good and positive impact of these activities.

These displays are connected to various types of competitions announcement by the library and faculty members. Such as book review, short story writing, translations, Seminars, poem writing, essay writing competitions are conducted on the basis of these displays. The competitions are open to all the students of college for the participation. These competitions contribute to enhance students' analytical skills, critical thinking skill, presentations skill and many more qualities that students required to face academic and professional challenges in their life. Apart from this library also organizes in-house book displays based on observations of various important days and events. During the Departmental seminars and conferences departmental book displays are conducted keeping in mind the theme of seminar. The response for this display by the students and staff members is very positive and motivating.

SMILOGRAM CARD

Every year on the basis of evaluation of student's performance in the examination and their use of library best library user award awarded to the students. This award includes Smilogram card, this card holders get the privilege of borrowing one extra book from the library throughout the academic year. This practice encourages students for optimum utilization of library.

CAREER CORNER

This is very informative corner for the students, as this corner is created by keeping in mind the objective to make students aware or inform them about upcoming and existing professions. Also this corner gives them information about the qualification and expertise they are required to face the competition of external world. For instance information related to various central and state government vacancies and how to prepare for different competitive exams, information regarding that are displayed over here.

STUDY SKILL BOARD

This is the area where skills required for preparation of different types of examinations are displayed. For instance how to learn content, techniques of memorization the things and revision styles are displayed over here. Junior college students very much benefited through this board.

WEBOPAC

Webopac has been installed in the library and through online library catalogue access to the library collection provided by 24*7 to the staff members and students of the college.

USER MANUAL

In order to make library more users friendly and to provide easy and simple access to library collection BCCA library has displayed one user manual at the entrance of the library. User manual is a written document which gives information about guidelines for library catalogue search (webopac), list of classification numbers with subject, borrowing procedure, important library rules, and library membership details, special features of library collection along with the list of subscribed journals, and list of subscribed newspapers also provided.

COMPUTER AND INTERNET SERVICES

Computers with an N-computing facility provided to the staff and students with internet connection. Students are allowed to use the internet for educational purpose at a nominal charge.

SPECIAL FEATURES OF THE LIBRARY

BCCA library has a rich collection of Urdu, Arabic and Islamic literature. A sound collection can be found in subjects like Psychology, English and Economics. Library has some treasured, rare books too.

CONCLUSION

Being a academic librarian we need to become more vocal, active and more involve with the educational process in order to meet the challenges ahead in the contemporary era. Library should be continues to fulfill its role as the heart of institution by contributing directly to the institutions academic mission and to equipping students with the skills and knowledge they need to achieve academically and to maximize their employment opportunity.

However, the most important role the academic librarian can take on is that of partner to, or collaborator with, teaching faculty. Without the involvement of faculty, the objectives of student's academic as well as professional development may not be achieved. Best practices never are the best practices if it is not contributing to the student's well being, if it is not contributing in creation of culturally literate community and nation.

REFERENCES

The value of academic libraries Retrieved on 21/01/2015 from *http://www.sconul.ac.uk/page/the-value-of-academic-libraries*

Sheridan, D. (2002). Combining teaching and library work: the hybrid academic. Liber Quarterly 12, 175-184.

Allen, L. (2000). Information literacy in higher education: a revolution in learning Retrieved on 21/01/2015 from http://www.pages.drexel.edu/~la35/information_literacy_in_higher_education.html.

16

Best Practices of SMRK-BK-AK Mahila Mahavidyalaya, Library, Nashik

S. A. Kulkarni

Librarian, SMRK-BK-AK Mahila Mahvidyalaya,
Prin. T. A. Kulkarni Vidyanagar, Nashik-422005.

ABSTRACT

The present paper described the best practices and their importance in higher education. This paper elaborated best practices followed by SMRK-BK-AK Mahila Mahavidyalaya, Nashik-5 in concern with major library features that is, Management and Administration, Finance, Staff, Facilities and Services.

Keywords : best practices, best practices in higher education, best practices in college library

INTRODUCTION

India has a wide range of variation and complexity from region to region. There are geographic diversities, differences in physical environment, ethic multitude and socio-economic disparities as well as intensified demographic pressures. These factors are reflects on the various issues of the Higher Education Institutions at various levels. Indian higher education system has a mix of all kinds of institutions with respect to quality. Among those one can find institutions of higher standards, average and below average.

Quality assurance is totally an integral part of all higher education systems. With the internationalization of higher education, quality has become a global issue and many countries are demanding international standards in higher education. The impulse is for the adoption of benchmarks that are acceptable to stakeholders nationally, and preferably globally.

DEFINITION

"Best practices are the best way to perform a business process, or an activity within a process that leads to superior performance within any field of endeavor."

Best Practices Benchmarking can be summarized as the:

- Development of an understanding of the fundamentals that lead to success,
- Focus on continuous improvement efforts and
- Management of the overall change process to close the gap between existing practices of the institutions with reference to the most relevant key performance variables.

Stella A, (2003) stresses the point that for quality assessment and enhancement, best practices benchmarking is the best alternative.

BEST PRACTICES BENCHMARKING IN HIGHER EDUCATION

Benchmarking 'best practice' as a means for continuous improvement through sustainable innovations is familiar in the world of business management. In recent years, this approach is also being adopted in many fields, including higher education.

Benchmarking through best practices is not a new concept in higher education. It has already been tried by the ACU (Association of Commonwealth Universities) through CHEMS (Commonwealth Higher Education Management Service) in 1996. According to CHEMS methodology, it is this process that the University Management Benchmarking Club encapsulates true benchmarking i.e. in the absence of predetermined benchmarks; the aim is to establish benchmarks through the process. Many organizations are coming up with their 'best practices database' to demonstrate in practical ways, what actually works in nourishing quality efforts. (Prasad V.S. and Stella Antony, 2004)

The NAAC has introduced a methodology similar to that of CHEM's. Only the difference is that rather than compiling best practices as stated by the Higher Education Institutions (HEIs) the NAAC would like to validate them and include in its database only those that are beneficial in the judgment of the peers. Emphasizing the need to reflect on best practices, the NAAC intends to make the identification and validation of best practices as a part of the re-accreditation strategy.

PROCESS OF BEST PRACTICE

Best practice is a continuous process followed by any institution like college library. For the action plan of the best practice in the college library following components should be considered.

BEST PRACTICES OF SMRK-BK-AK MAHILA MAHAVIDYALAYA, LIBRARY

Management and Administration

It is a responsibility of college librarian to carry out all activities in a scheduled time and without or minimum help of the supporting staff.

- Academic calendar for every college is mandatory as per NAAC requirement. Involvement of library programmes in this academic calendar creates importance of library activates.
- Work distribution chart of all personals of the library displays each and every job of library performed. This chart shows picture of library staff as well as which type of activates related to library and other than library performed with time.
- Library applies Pocket system for circulation. Membership Card and Stock Taking Card uses for maintain and preserve data. Library professionals are use to the card filling therefore; this data related activities are performing in minimum staff and time. These also save space.
- According to requirement library prepared formats of various documents that are: Book Recommendation, Monthly Factual data of Usages, Appraisal of Library Services by Students and staff, Annual Library Report, Library Rules and Regulations.

Library Finance

- Library yearly prepare faculty wise and subject wise budget allocation and execute purchasing accordingly.
- Library appeal to the members to donate books or amount deposited as library deposit and rise funds as well as collection.
- User friendly approach, personal assistance helps effectiveness of paying facilities like photo coping, Internet surfing. This raises funds.

Library Staff

- Innovative activities and programmes organize by library with the students sharing this performs activity with inadequate staff.
- Identify the skills/soft skills of illiterate and non professional supporting staff and delegate some work accordingly to them. Sincerity and hard work of supporting staff performs various type of technical/mechanical work like good handwriting man can prepare various lists, cards this helps to maintain data, scanning for digitization and depositories.
- Pocket system and barcode makes easier circulation by unprofessional supporting staff.

Library Facilities and Services

- Various displays arrange regularly.
- For studious and sincere students providing advance learner facility and giving additional book, excuse for late fees etc.
- Library provides additional book pocket to Book Club member students and Competitive Exam Guidance Cell members.
- Registration for Alumni Association performs continuous interaction with former students helps

for institutional linkages.

- Library performed MOU's with well known other libraries in the city and strengthen Inter Library Cooperation.
- Suggestion box is available with timely response and periodical user study, helps to assess and improve library practice.
- Library day celebrates on 27th September on death anniversary of Dr. S. R. Ranganathan, Father of Library science, with innovative competitions, quiz and exhibition.
- For interactive service made available through Blog i.e. *www.smrklibraryblogspot.com*
- Knowledge Buzz, Question Paper Archive, Important quick links, New Arrivals, News Paper Clippings these are the main features of this link. Through Faculty Comment students can interact with their faculty and get information on curriculum, important topics etc. this increases the usages of library.

CONCLUSION

To satisfy our users and stakeholders and improve our quality in changing environment we are adopting more and more best practices. We are looking forward towards leading college libraries as a benchmarking and trying to perform for quality excellence.

REFERENCES

- Kulkarni S.A. (2009), Best Practices in College Libraries, a paper published in proceeding of the National Seminar, Library and Information Services in Changing Era, Univ. of Pune, Pune, Jan 22-23, 2009, pp273-281.
- Quality Procedures Mannual (ISO9001; 2008), College Library, SMRK-BK-AK Mahila Mahavidyalaya, Nasik (Unpublished).

17

User Centric Best Practices of Khandwala College Library

Santosh C. Hulagabali
Librarian, Nagindas Khandwala College,
Malad (W), Mumbai-400 064

ABSTRACT

The Khandwala College Library's innovative initiatives focus on users of its institution as well as the users of different academic institutes. It follows an open policy to share the information helpful for research and teaching activities. The Library's efforts in attracting the user base to its innovative services are well received. Right from automation to stock verification, from certificate course for researchers to launching an abstracting database of conference papers for educators/researchers, from training librarians to researchers, many innovative activities are being carried out. The paper shares details about selected innovative initiatives carried out by Khandwala College Library.

Keywords: *Best Practices, Khandwala College Library, ICon-AD, COIST*

1. INTRODUCTION

The Khandwala College Library's services and activities revolve around its users. User and their needs are the top priorities of the Library. As customer is considered a king in business, the Library considers its user a king as the success of the Library and its services are greatly dependent on the users. The Library's innovative initiatives are a passionate approach and attempt to go beyond the routine library and information services. All the healthy practices discussed in this paper are those that have impacted users, image and credibility of the Library in myriad ways.

In this paper, each practice is presented under four sub-heads viz. (a) Practice- that introduces the best practice and its basic features; b) Process- that shares the pre-and post implementation tasks of the practices; c) Outcome- that reveals the evidence of success of the practice. d) Future Plan- that envisages the target to be achieved with the respective best practice.

2. ABOUT KHANDWALA COLLEGE

Nagindas Khandwala College, Malad (W), Mumbai, one of the best Colleges of University of Mumbai, is imparting quality education from last four decades. The College is affiliated to University of Mumbai and reaccredited by UGC-NAAC with 'A' Grade (3rd Cycle). It runs courses ranging from graduation to Ph.D with around four thousand students and nearly hundred skilled and experienced teaching faculty with active supporting staff. The College has all necessary educational infrastructures. Being an ISO 9001:2008 certified educational institute, it is also one of the Lead Colleges of University of Mumbai. It has bagged many prestigious awards including IMC Ramkrishna Bajaj Award, BEQET Award, Education Excellence Award of Indus Foundation Inc., USA, and Best College status conferred by University of Mumbai for the year 2012-13.

3. ABOUT KHANDWALA COLLEGE LIBRARY

The Library and Information Centre is one of the state-of-the art College libraries in the western suburbs of Mumbai. The Library is instrumental in impacting large number of students, researchers, educators and trainers serving in and out of the College. Rich with qualitative collection of kind of documents, the Library is fully automated with latest library functionalities, technologies and equipments. The following best practices further introduce the Library and its activities.

4. USER CENTRIC BEST PRACTICES

4.1. Certificate Programme for Research Scholars (COIST)

1. Practice : The Library undertakes teaching and training activities for the researchers and post graduate students of different colleges and universities. A short-term Certificate Programme for research scholars i.e. Certificate Course in Online Information Sources, Tools and Techniques (COIST) was introduced in 2013. The course is open to all but preference is given to the research scholars pursuing research degrees. The Course is being conducted twice in an academic year.

2. Process : The COIST imparts an extensive training on online information sources, tools and techniques for researchers. The scope, syllabus and teaching method are planned and executed with the help and advice from the LIS experts and senior educators. The official website (http://www.coist.weebly.com) of COIST was hosted with sufficient information about the course curriculum, eligibility criteria, fees, resource persons, online admission procedures etc. The classes are conducted on five Saturdays for four hours a day. The classes are engaged by noted information professionals working in premiere academic institutes of Mumbai and adjacent cities. The programme is practical in nature and each participant appears for a test of hundred marks at the end of the programme. The grade-based certificates are awarded to the successful candidates.

3. Outcome : The Course is well received by the researchers as the response is astounding. So far the Library has successfully completed three batches and trained thirty two researchers of different domains and universities. It is found that the researchers mastered the art of exploring the scholarly literature online. The course has immensely helped their research work and publication activities. Interestingly, many of the researchers who successfully completed the Course contact the Library staff often to discuss their queries or learn more on the issues discussed in the Course.

Information professionals and experts have appreciated the initiative. Dr. R Guruprasad, Scientist, KTMD, CSIR-National Aerospace Laboratories (NAL) says "This course which is of immense value to a Ph.D. research scholar or even a Post Doctor as being aware of online e-resources, tools and content building software are extremely important." (personal communication via e-mail, November 11, 2013). And Dr. Neha Chaudhari, Centre for Internet and Society opines "The course is a wonderful idea. The course outline seems very comprehensive." (personal communication via e-mail, November 11, 2013).

4. Future Plan : A similar course shall be introduced for research guides of different domains and universities in the academic year 2015-16.

4.2. Indian Conference-Abstracting Database (ICon-AD)

1. Practice : The ICon-AD is a non-profit initiative and a growing database of abstracts of papers presented at conferences held in India. The ICon-AD was conceived keeping the status of Indian conferences and publication trends in mind. It is observed that not all conference organisers publish the conference proceedings. Publishing conference papers holds importance because conferences always focus on the ongoing or futuristic trends of a particular domain (Hulagabali, 2014).

2. Process : The aim was to share the topics/papers that were discussed in the conferences and also to connect the readers with the authors to exchange the scholarly information. After the successful installation of DSpace (an open source software), the data of some selected conference abstracts were fed. With rigorous testing and rearrangement of the data according to the fields given by DSpace, the beta version of ICon-AD was launched on 1st January, 2014.

The organisers of various conferences were then contacted. The utilities of the project were shared with them and requested them to share the conference abstracts. The abstracts were collected with a formal agreement to share the abstracts for the larger interest of the readers. Each abstract was then formatted with ICon-AD's style sheet and converted in pdf file-format. Metadata entries were fed in the database and sufficient information about the conference, its organiser and the organising secretary's details were added. The archival of abstract is one of the routine activities of the Library staff as we are receiving increasing number of abstracts from the conference organisers.

3. Outcome : The response was overwhelming from the conference organsiers. The database helped form collaboration with twenty two academic institutes that came forward and shared their conference abstracts. As of 1st February, 2015, the database comprises 1220 abstracts (of 30 conferences) written by 1597 authors. The biggest evidence of success of this practice is that Google Scholar is indexing ICon-AD entries. Readers can now search and find abstracts form Google Scholar too. On the other hand, the database has helped the authors to have a strong online presence with their academic contributions and that is attracting many more readers.

Information professionals and experts have appreciated the initiative. Nevena Tomic, Library Manager, Students' City Cultural Center, Serbia says "It is an interesting archive and valuable resource." (personal communication via Linkedin, September 9, 2014). And Dr. Marianne Bamkin (of OpenDOAR's), Centre for Research Communications, Nottingham University says "It appears to be an interesting archive and valuable resource" (personal communication via e-mail, June 23, 2014).

4. Future Plan : Efforts will be made to incorporate the conference abstracts of reputed institutes like IIM and IIT; funding and sponsoring bodies (for conferences) like ICSSR, UGC, DST etc. and research institutes like TIFR, BARC, ISEC, IGIDR, NAL etc.

4.3. Earn While You Learn Scheme (EWYLS)

1. Practice : The EWYLS is started in 2011-12 and is one of the popular best practices of the Library. The students are much familiar with this scheme as they have been seeing their seniors working in different departments of the College (under this scheme). Any student studying in second or third year of graduation and wishing to pursue a part-time job in the different departments of the College (including Library) can apply for the scheme. Five students are recruited every year. The selected students are required to work for four man-hours a day in respective section of the College and offered monthly stipend.

2. Process : Teachers introduce the EWYLS in the classes at the beginning of the College. Students obtain complete details about the scheme from the Library staff too. Desirous students submit written application to the Librarian. After initial scrutiny, the students are informed to appear for Aptitude Test that comprises MCQs and also few descriptive questions ranging from general knowledge to current affairs. Post-test, the selected students are called for group-discussion and interview. The list of successful students is posted on the website and they are placed in different departments.

3. Outcome : Students working in different departments of the College understand the functionality of an education institute. Their perception of their own College becomes more positive as they see it being an employee as well as a student. Their innovative ideas and noteworthy contributions also helps improve the system.

4. Future Plan : Providing part-time job opportunity to more number of students with formal training programmes from the corporate trainers and educators. It is also planned to start 'Sponsor a Trainee' scheme to provide stipend to the selected students working under the scheme.

4.4. Training cum Mutual Learning Programme (TMLP)

1. Practice : Many librarians and researchers of different institutes access our library. The queries and consultations of these user categories are different. To make this assistance more formal, we introduced the TMLP. This initiative helps learning the best things about each other's library mutually. As regard to research scholars, training them on effective use of different sources of information especially online information sources is necessary. With this observation, the TMLP was devised and is being conducted preferably on any Saturday based on the demand from the librarians and researchers.

2. Process : The librarians/researchers need to contact the Librarian with queries. Depending upon the scope of the queries, the discussion (on any Saturday) is arranged. The discussions are recorded and feedback from the participant is taken. The event details are then enumerated in the Library records as well as posted on the Library's blog.

3. Outcome : Catering voluntary assistance to the researchers and librarians became formal through TMLP initiative. The prominent outcome of TMLP is two dimensional. Firstly, researchers' complex queries help us study, review and serve them well with the required solutions. Secondly, both librarians and researchers help us know what way we need to develop our system, improve services and sharpen knowledge too. This initiative was a learning curve for us as it helped us conduct training in a formal and effective way. Moreover, it helped us plan and conduct the training, prepare training documentation, analyze our strength and scope for improvement etc. Such approaches constantly help us in showcasing our initiatives to inspecting bodies.

4. Future Plan : To conduct more number of training prorammes on regular basis and also inviting senior information professionals to train the librarians and researchers.

4.5. Miscellaneous Practices

The Library believes that every library ought to have its Library Social Responsibility (LSR) for serving the academic and social community directly or indirectly. Following healthy practices try to achieve the same.

1. Association with Voluntary Libraries : The Library and its staff associate themselves with some non-profit voluntary organisations that are instrumental in starting and maintaining libraries for the public. For instance: a pilot study on such libraries, located in Mumbai and Thane districts, was undertaken to know the libraries' working condition. Personal visits by the Librarian and some student volunteers were made to around twenty plus such libraries. Connecting with these libraries helped us share our ideas on latest technology available for libraries, documentation methods, information marketing skills, undertaking use and user studies, stock taking methods, etc. The visits to these libraries are being made as and when the libraries need any assistance from us.

2. Discussion Forum for Researchers: Understanding the need of a platform for research scholars to share their queries related to their research, research policies/guidelines, current trends, job openings, training programmes, ongoing discussions, forthcoming conferences etc., the Library launched online discussion forum i.e. Indian Forum of Research Scholars in Social Sciences (IFRSSS). More than six hundred researchers, educators and librarians mutually and actively participate in the discussions and share information. This initiative helped us learn various different information needs of researchers that are different from the users of other categories.

3. Research Reference Services : The library offers free membership to research scholars (of University of Mumbai and its affiliated colleges) pursuing doctoral degrees. The service is catered against the official request (letter issued) by the research supervisor or librarian of their institute to avail the said service. More than fifteen to twenty researchers are using this service every year.

4. Inter Library Loan (ILL) : The Library offers ILL for the libraries located in the adjacent localities of the College. Based on the written application by the librarian or head of the institute of the participating library, two books are issued for one month. This benefits us in maintaining the professional relation with other libraries.

Apart from the above healthy practices, following are some of the selected best practices of Khandwala College Library.

5. In-house Printing of Borrowers' Cards : As stated before, the Library is fully automated with library management software and other latest technology. The Library staff prepares the borrowers' cards (with barcode) in the Library itself by using a multi-colour printer. The staff are trained to handle the database as well the printing of cards. The colour ribbons, PVC cards, barcode labels and cleaning kits are being used to print the cards. This move has helped us in issuing cards to students on time and save money as outsourcing of the same work would cost us more.

6. Document Archive and Management : The acquisition section is equipped with scanners. The Library assistants scan every invoice at the time of processing the books. The scanned invoices are codified (with the date of invoice, vendor, subject and course codes) to maintain uniformity and easy retrieval for future use. The Library assistants are also scanning and archiving syllabus copies and old question papers. Both the documents are accessible to students from our Internet facility centre. Students can download and share them with their fellow classmates. This has avoided repeated requests for hard copies of question papers and syllabus copies and also helped avoid improper handling of (the bunches of) question papers and syllabus copies.

7. Automated Stock Verification : The Library uses wireless mobile scanners while stock checking. The library staff takes the machine to the stack room and scans the barcodes of the books individually. The device works on Wi-Fi mode and can store ten thousand records. The accession numbers are beamed on the computer (note pad). Later the note pad, bearing the accession numbers, is imported to the database and the status is marked (against each scanned book) as 'on shelf'. This device is handy, user friendly and helps save time, energy, avoids duplication of efforts and also brings accuracy in the stock verification process.

8. Online Presence of the Library : Connecting with the users online is as important as meeting them in the Library every day. The focal objective, behind having a strong online presence of the Library, is to market our information services and thus create interest and awareness about the utilities among the users. Considering this, we started adding sufficient information about the Library, its services, facilities, list of best practices, library staff publications, online requisition form etc. on our College website (http://www.nkc.ac.in); we also created Library's official blog (http://www.nkcblogspot.com) in 2009; and also opened accounts in social networking sites. On behalf of the faculty, the Library adds the publication details of its faculty on Google Scholar and their selected PPTs on http://www.slideshare.net. It is also important to state that the Library manages the College's official website right from content development to updating the site. All these supportive online activities have helped boost the image of the Library as well as the College.

9. Project on our Library : We support our students (of BSc Information Technology and Computer Science) to undertake projects on our Library. For instance: students of IT and Computer Science compile programmes to design library software with basic modules. Moreover, many BLISc and MLISc students of different universities have undertaken project works on our Library as partial fulfillment of their degrees. Such research studies have helped us identify our limitations and improve the system.

10. Internship Programmes : The Library offers Internship and Training Programme for Library Science student/s and professionals. Every year we are training one M.L.I.Sc. student studying in Department of Library and Information Science, University of Mumbai for 15 days as Internship Programme at our Library. Such programmes are helping the Library staff to sharpen their training skills and provide the best possible training to the interns.

11. Students Participation in Decision Making : To involve students in decision making Student Library Advisor Committee (SLAC) is formed and the meeting of the same is conducted twice a year. The initiative has helped understand the students' issues related to the Library and address them constructively.

12. Language Learning Initiative : One third of the students need training on communication skills especially in English. The teachers are putting lot of efforts in improving students' learning ability in the said language. To support this from the Library, we issue books on grammar, essay and stories to the students. The students exchange the books and return them every month and take up new books. This results in gradual improvement in their learning, writing, reading and applying skills.

13. Online Requisition : Library is a democratic institute. Students of our Library are free to recommend any books to the Library. They can recommend the books online and the book/s is/are procured within eight working days (subject to availability). This initiative brings smile on the students' faces as they feel their requests are honoured by adding the book/s in the library.

14. Internet Facility Centre : Students can access Internet in the Library premises on designated computers for thirty minutes a day. The access period is extended if any computer is not occupied by any other student. The students are also free to access Internet on Wi-Fi mode. This Centre also helps the Library staff to orient the students (coming to Library for accessing the Internet) about various open access sources available online and the databases subscribed by the Library.

15. Publication : The Library publishes books and conference proceedings under the banner of Khandwala Publishing House (KPH), a publishing unit of our College. So far KPH has published four books.

5. CONCLUSION

The Khandwala College Library strives hard to sustain the above discussed initiatives. The practices are reviewed periodically to accommodate the necessary changes to make the initiatives more innovative and user centric. These practices have not only helped us in building a strong and active user base but also helped us in our studies, teaching and research activities. Though few of the above initiatives are general, we are admired and appreciated by our readers, faculty, management and also the users working in different institutes who are part of our services. The Library's aim is to build a library that supports learning, teaching, training, research and publication activities of the users. And the above initiatives are the testimony to it. Dr. R S Deshpande, Director of Institute of Social and Economic Change who gave his remark about our Library in the visitor's register as: "Khandwala College Library is equivalent to any good research institute's library" (personal communication, February 15, 2008). We feel this is an apt remark and we are putting every possible effort to achieve this status.

REFERENCE

Hulagabali, S. C. (2014). Building National Archive of Conference Abstracts: A Pilot Study on Indian Conference-Abstracting Database (ICon-AD). *International Journal of Information Resources and Knowledge Management*, 1 (2), 105.

18

ICT Based Best Practices & Innovations in Chhatrapati Shahu Ji Maharaj Centre for Studies of Maratha History Library

Kamble Ashwini Rajarm
Librarian, Shri. Shivajirao Deshmukh College of Education, Red-Shirala. Tal- Shirala Dist-Sangli

ABSTRACT

Library is part & Parcel of the every institution. We live in this ICT based information age and libraries are expected to use Information & communication Technology to provide nascent information more expeditiously & exhaustively. The success of the every library is depending upon its providing better services to meet the specific needs.

This paper discusses on the Best & ICT based practices practiced in the CSMCSMH Library, Shivaji University Kolhapur to enhance the academic information environment & publicize the available resource for the effective use by the faculty & students for their teaching. The centres try to become an advance centre for learning & research in Maratha History.

Keywords : ICT, CSMCSMH, Maratha History, Maratha Centre

INTRODUCTION

Before the ICT the libraries were the sole custodians of information which was predominately in print. ICT brought changes by new information repackaging. It means due to the ICT convergence of technologies came into significant changes in the scholarly information environment. Due to the technological changes library professionals have to acquire new skills, abilities and knowledge. The impact of web-based, the information atmosphere around the world is changing, it means every minute and growing at a tremendous speed. ICT globalization of network and Internet, & has influenced very much on every facets of library and information services. For automated production of catalogue cards, later for printed catalogs or paper. Gradually the potential of computers as the instrument of a totally new type of catalogue was understood, and the hard copy catalogue was replaced by OPAC.

Libraries are changing in terms of their collection, facilities and services owing to constant changing scenario of information due to ICT (Information Communication Technology) applications and information seeking behavior of the users. The Library apart from providing traditional library services in a computerized environment act as Learning Resource Centre.

1. Chh Shahu Maharaj Centre for Studies of Maratha History: A Profile

The Shivaji University in pursuit or one of its basic foundation objectives being exploration of studies in Maharashtra set up this Centre named after illustrious Chh. Shahu Maharaj in 2003 under the History department which was established on 9th November 1964. The department's main aim is to focusing on Indian History with emphasis on the history of the Marathas. The department credit goes to the several valuable research publications mainly in Maratha History and

Southern Maratha Country States. Many research projects funded by national agencies like UGC & ICHR (Indian Council of Historical Research), New Delhi. Due to continuous research activities in Maratha History were acknowledged by the Maharashtra State Govt. by approving the establishment of Chhatrapati Shahu Maharaj Centre for Studies of Maratha History.

It is said that, "This Centre is in fact **offshoot** of the History dept.".

1.1. Vission & Mission-

1. Vission : Initiation, promotion & co-ordination of Multi-Dementia Research in Maratha History in particular and that Deccan in general.

2. Mission : To create research awareness among young generation & extend it.

Training in source languages scripts such as Modi, Persian, Portuguese, etc.

2. OBJECTIVES OF THE STUDY

1. To identify the best practices
2. To study ICT based practices followed by CSMCSMH.

3. LIMITATION OF THE STUDY

This study of the ICT based practices is limited in Chh. Shahu Maharaj Centre for Studies of Maratha History's Library.

4. CSMCSMH LIBRARY

Every Library is the lung of every education institute. The collection of special or departmental libraries may contain many rare & valuable materials. It also may or may not be accessible to some identified part of the general public. The Chh. Shahu Maharaj Centre for Studies of Maratha History collections which is majorly donated by Dr. A.R. Kulkarni & A.R. Bhosale sir & those are rare books. These rare source materials for the studies of Maratha History is available in Digitized form & also in print form, CD-ROM's. It means the library holds donated 600 books & totally 193 periodicals. The centre has procured 612 CD's containing 3,50,000 (Three lack fifty thousand) Primary manuscripts on Maratha History from the Govt.of Maharashtra State Achieves Pune & Mumbai which are totally modi documents.

ICT BASED BEST PRACTICES & INNOVATIONS IN CSMCSMH LIBRARY

4.1. As An Asset

The History department supposed to this Centre as an Asset. It is the only centre in India which undertakes research related to the studies in Maratha History with State, National & International recognition.

4.2. Research Areas

Maratha History, History of Modern Maharashtra & History of Southern Maratha Country are thrust areas of the department. To set up the centre for Historical Studies, Research & Cultural Heritage in SUK in course of time is our cherished goal. The Maratha Centre provides consultancy service to general public regarding old modi documents.

5. E-LIBRARY SETUP

5.1. Broadband Internet Connectivity-

The Centre has separate connection of broadband internet connectivity to supply the services to the faculty member & students.

5.2. Excellent facility of E-Library

The Library has excellent facility of E-Library equipped with microfilm reader, microfilm scanner, document camera.

6. INSTITUTIONAL REPOSITORY SOFTWARE

An Institutional Repository is an online locus for collecting & preserving in digital form the intellectual output of an institution particularly research institutions. IRS are partly linked to the notion of a digital library. i.e collecting, housing,classifying, cataloguing, curating, preserving & providing access to digital content analogous with the libraries conventional function of collecting, housing, classifying, curating preserving & providing access to analog content.

6.1. Dspace

The Centre installed for the digitization the 'Dspace' open source digital library management software which was developed by MIT (Massachusetts Institute of Technology) libraries & Hewlett-Packard labs. It runs on Linux & Apache web Server, Tomcat Servlet enging & the Postgre SQL relational database system.

Totally rare books in digital form & also Dspace preserves & enable easy & open access to all types of historical digital content including text, Conference's, news clipping, images, various Maharajas mpegs & data sets.

This Dspace is an ever-growing community of developers, committed to continuously expanding and improving the software, each Dspace installation benefits from the next.

6.2. Library Users

The books & non books materials preserved in the centre library are issued to the researcher enrolled with the Shivaji University for pursuing M.Phil, Ph.D. doctoral degrees & for other bonafide researcher on requisition.

6.3. Library Staff

The centre has the staff which has totally on 11 months contract basis. Library holds 1 Coordinator, 2

Research Assistant, 1 Librarian, 1 Stenographer, 1 Peon.

6.4. Tools for Acquisition

The library uses bibliography, expert's opinion, coordinator's opinion & purchase committee remarks & purchase committee remarks, students or researchers recommendations regarding research.

6.5. Library Opening & Closing Hours

Centre library open from Monday to Saturday morning 10.20 a.m. to evening 6.00 p.m. & the library will be closed on the Govt. holiday.

6.6. Access Services

CSMCSMH library is a mixture of both as it contains a historical collection for circulation & a rare collection which is often more specialized as well as restrict to the library premises.

6.7. Organization of the Collection

6.7.1. Classification

The centre has used the co-operative classification or with the help of BBKL's Web OPAC for referencing classification.

6.7.2. Documents Cataloguing

The Centre has used or maintain the documents cataloguing by the Dspace software.

6.8. Financial Management

Primary source of library funds that the university provide every year 1,00,000/- for maintain the library &center development & second source means the some eminent or professor historical lovers are donate rare copies which are not easily available today. Some people donate Modi documents which will be preserved in this center as a rare source material.

6.9. Library Lending Services

The centre is providing the following services

1. SDI Service
2. Reprographic service
3. Newspaper Clipping Service
4. Inter Library Loan Service
5. OPAC
6. Reference Service
7. Consultancy Service

7. SPECIAL BEST PRACTICES

CSMCSMH Library conducting the Certificate Course in Modi Script. The faculty members of Research Assistant provide consultancy service to general public regarding old modi documents. This consultancy is of course free of charge.

8. FUTURE PLAN

1. To edit rare historical source material for publication
2. To create strong infrastructure in the form of computer & printer
3. Expansion of departmental library to facilitate more students.
4. To procure primary sources for Maratha Studies from Libraries.

CONCLUSION

Library is mean or a support to achieve the goal & objectives of the institution. The Chh. Shahu Maharaj Centre for Studies of Maratha History has a well-equipped library with an elaborated collection of books, journals, project reports, A-V material, e-books, CD-ROM to serve its users.

Through the library database easily accessible data which is beneficial for the research purposes & the database are made available to the scholars for their further reference.

REFERENCES

1. Agar, J. K.; Volans, J. K. S.;&-Runcie, K.V. (1984). Managing information to fit thenet.d. *Journal* of *Information Sczence,* 8(5),22. pp.5-227
2. Abubakar, A. (2003) College of education libraries: the need for more emphasis on user education. *Isa Kaita Multidisciplinary Journal of Education,*V.1(1):pp.15-20.
3. HistoryDept. Profile.
4. Kenneth Crews, (2011).The Academic Library in the Information Age: Changing Roles. California State University, A CETUS Publication Series p. 8-28.
5. Lal C. & Kumar K. (2010). Descriptive Questions in Library & Information Science, Ess Ess Publication, New Delhi; pp.380.
6. Shashi Prabha Singh, Veralkshmi R.S.R.(2012).Cloud computing: A Promising Economic Model for Library and Information Centres. *DESIDOC Journal of Library & Information Technology,*32(6) p. 526-53
7. *www.dspace.org* (last accessed dated on 04 Dec.2014 09.00 a.m.)
8. Yoo-Seong Song.(2009). Designing library services based on user needs: newopportunities to re-position the library. *WORLD LIBRARY AND INFORMATION CONGRESS: 75TH IFLA GENERAL CONFERENCE AND COUNCIL* 23-27 August 2009, Milan, Italy.pp.01.

19

Best Practices in Academic Libraries with Special Reference to the Chakdaha College Library, Nadia, West Bengal: An Empirical Study

Ranjan Karmakar
Librarian, Chakdaha College,
Chakdaha, Nadia, West Bengal.

ABSTRACT

Role of libraries in the era of information explosion in 21st century is very important. Library tries to provide maximum service provide to students, staff, and external readers in minimum cost. The global changes particularly the Information and Communication Technologies (ICT) have impact on the functioning of academic libraries. Government of India, UGC and NAAC are seriously concerned regarding how to improve standards of education and establish best practices in the universities and colleges and their libraries. In the process of institutional accreditation, libraries play a crucial role. Library is the fulcrum of support for the entire range of academic activities on an educational campus. It is true that libraries largely support learning, teaching and research processes in institutions. It defines best practices as an application of procedures to yield superior results which means way of doing things in particular organization as guidelines for good practices. Explains NAAC's concern for quality of library practices as well as NACC's set of best practices in academic libraries. The Paper throws light with the introduction and have stated the current status of the library of Chakdaha College collection development. Lastly the article stresses on the best practices in the Chakdaha College library, i.e. Library Services to external readers, Internet Facility in the Library, Book Bank Facility and Information about Competitive Exams. In this paper author tries to take review of these best practices adopted by Chakdaha College Library.

Keywords : Best Practices, Academic Libraries, Library Services, Digital Services, UGC, NAAC, Chakdaha College.

INTRODUCTION

"The kind of education given to the library profession is normally reflected in the service given by the profession." — ***Dr. S. R. Ranganathan***

Education aims to impart knowledge and makes good citizens. Libraries are the repositories of knowledge and form an integral part of education. Libraries have a long history, starting with the chained and closed-access libraries of earlier times to the present-day hybrid, digital, and virtual libraries that use the latest technology for provision of information through various services. Accordingly, librarians have also changed from storekeepers who were concerned with protection of books against theft, mutilation, and pilferage, to that of information officers, navigators, and cybrarians who find themselves in the vast ocean of reading material and are busy in satisfying their clients who want anytime and anywhere information (Mahajan, 2005).

The global changes particularly the present Information and Communication Technologies (ICT) have made the nature of libraries has changed dramatically and a tremendous impact on the functions of the academic libraries. Computers are being used in libraries to process, store, retrieve and disseminate information. As a result, the traditional concept of library is being redefined from a place to access books to one which houses the most advanced media including CD-ROM, Internet, and remote access to a wide range of resources. Libraries have now metamorphosed into digital institutions. The developments and changes in ICT have changed the users' expectation from the academic libraries in different ways. Gone are the days when a library was judged by its quantitative resources. Today, libraries are surrounded by networked data that is connected to a vast ocean of Internet-based service. Moreover, electronic resources relevant to the professions are developing at an unprecedented pace. The ways to build a library collection and offer services to the end users vary from the recent to past exercises. To meet the end-users demands effectively, the academic libraries need to identify and adopt good practices and benchmarks, which will ultimately enhance the value based services of the libraries in an academic environment. Thus, preparing guidelines in a standardized way based on the best practices employed by libraries is significant which will ultimately enhance the value based services of academic libraries (Umesh, 2012).

Academic libraries are considered to be the nerve centres of academic institutions, and must support teaching, research, and other academic programmes. The situation in academic libraries of India is the same as that of academic libraries the world over; however, Indian libraries must provide maximum information with limited resources. Colleges form the integral part of Higher education and libraries in colleges are the primary source for learning process. The college library is a connecting link between teaching and learning as well as place which supplements its resources what is beyond scope of class room. College libraries play an important role in the educational history of both the students as well as the faculty members. It serves the user by providing specific information to the user. But how far the college libraries are successful in implementing their goals into its reality is a big question. There must be some agency to have a proper vigilance on the functioning of college libraries and also to suggest certain measures to rectify the emerging needs, and for this kind of purpose NAAC was established for maintaining quality education of the institutions (Ahemad, & Pal, 2012).

In the process of institutional accreditation, libraries play a crucial role. The services of the libraries have been expanding as they contribute significantly to the learning process, particularly the e-learning process. Library is the fulcrum of support for the entire range of academic activities on an educational campus. In today's high-tech learning environment, the library as a learning resource is taking up increasingly more academic space and time in the life of a learner. In times ahead, this will be even more so. All this play up the need for scientific evaluation of a library so that its role as the centerpiece of academic development is protected and enhanced. It is true that libraries largely support learning, teaching and research processes in institutions (Wadje, 2012).

BACKGROUND: HISTORICAL PERSPECTIVE AND RESEARCH CONTEXT

Look at the history of higher education in India we find that Radhakrishnan (1948) and Kothari (1964) Commission Reports have already recognized the role of libraries in higher education. They had recommended the need of a first class library for the college and universities. Moreover UGC Library Committee Report (1965) headed by Dr. S. R. Ranganathan provided firm base to academic libraries. INFLIBNET since its inception in 1989 has been providing financial support to the academic libraries to automate library operations. Today INFLIBNET claims that it has supported more than 150 universities for library automation. It is hoped that within a decade almost all the universities will have library automation. However our journey towards college libraries is long, and shall take time to cover all the colleges of the country. National Knowledge Commission Report (2007) also realizes the significance or the role of different types of libraries (Vyas, 2009; and UGC, September, 2013).

Library and Information Services of Higher Education institutions play a central role in enhancing the quality of academic and research environment. Library is the fulcrum of support for the entire range of academic activities on an educational campus. In today's high-tech learning environment, the library as a learning resource is taking up increasingly more academic space and time in the life of a learner. In times ahead, this will be even more so. Several factors are forcing academic libraries to change. The drivers of change include social and economical factors which affect higher education in general and libraries in particular. The main three factors behind the change are changes in literate habits, changes in students and the curriculum, and changes in the technological infrastructure. Globalization is playing major role in making today's students more focused and demanding. At the same time it is introducing resource crunches and concept of value for money even in education sector. In this scenario, only those libraries can excel and satisfy its users which can develop best practices with the available resources (Kamble, & Tikam, 2010).

University Grants Commission has been striving for ensuring quality of higher education since its inception, and more so during last two decades. There has been tremendous surge in educational institutions coming up particularly after creation of All India Council of Technical Education AICTE in 1987. The surge is more in private sector which has opened flood gates in private sector institutions. Number of deemed universities and colleges which have come up recently needs assessment by higher educations experts. Now-a-days it has become a fashion to have a college of engineering and medical sciences. Norms have been flouted with impunity and how technical colleges are approved by AICTE is open secret (Vyas, 2009; and UGC, September, 2013).

LITERATURE REVIEW

It is recommended that NAAC should hold a National Seminar on Best Practices in academic libraries every year. The participation in the conference should be by paper presentation. Selection of papers for presentation is subject to peer review. Academic libraries are part of the large academic bodies. Generation, organization and dissemination of information and knowledge are subject to constant change since 1980s. Most academic libraries have the facility of Internet resources which supplement the print collection of the library. These changes are substantial. The problem with us is that many changes we come across, we immediately take it as a part of routine. Internet facility helps in saving time, repetition and redundancy, time lag and delays. We can communicate with information service providers within no time in case of any problem, change or adding new things to existing collection or services. Library management has to become more integrated through software. Librarians will have to study the potential of library software as many features are still not known to us (Vyas, 2009; and UGC, 2013).

NAAC in its publication Library and Information Services: Case Presentation (NAAC, 2006) explained its efforts towards quality. Prof. A. C. Tikekar's comment about the examples of best practices given under four significant areas of LIS "are from a very few and stray and from of the same universities and colleges. Some of them are very peripheral and not of core nature. It is a matter of discussion that the institutions included in the list are the only the best academic libraries. The name of the colleges and universities listed are not well known except few" (Tikekar, 2009; and Vyas, 2009).

Peter Brophy's The Library in the Twenty-first Century: New Services for the Information Age has devoted one chapter on "what is a good library" explains how researchers and patrons view 'goodness' in the library. A library in order to survive should acquire resources which are useful to users in present as well as these will be in future too. The question of goodness is not only related to efficiency and effectiveness of the process, but also adaptability and responsiveness of the library to its environment. Different organizations have different set of indicators to judge the quality of the library. And these indicators should have amalgam of both-traditional library operations and ICT base services. It is a subject of further research to find out how a library preference can be measured (Brophy, 2007).

THE EDUCATIONAL SYSTEM OF INDIA

India has a large higher education system. The growth rate of educational institutions in India was very slow before independence in 1947. Today there are a total of 700 universities, including general, science and technology, open, agricultural, women's, language and medical universities along with more than 35,000 affiliated colleges enrolling more than 29 million students, that provide education in all disciplines. Indian higher education is a large and complex system. The structure of degree-granting institutions is cumbersome primarily due to "affiliation" and funding sources. More than 85% of students are enrolled in bachelor's degree programs with majority enrolling in three-year B.A., B.Com. or B.Sc. degrees. One-sixth of all Indian students are enrolled in Engineering / Technology degrees (Choudaha, August, 2013; and India Education, December, 2014).

According to latest statistics provided by present UGC Chairman the capacity expansion in higher education has increased manifold which is evident from the following figures (University Grants Commission (UGC), June, 2013):

Table 1: The Educational System of India

Growth / Academic	*1950*	*2008*	*2014*
Universities	25	431	700
Colleges	700	20,677	35,539
Teachers	15000	5.05 Lakhs	9.51 lakhs (Out of 9.51 lakhs teachers, 82.54% teachers are in colleges and the remaining 17.46% in universities.)
Students	1.00 Lakhs	111.6 Lakhs	296.29 lakhs

Source: (UGC, June, 2013).

ROLE OF THE ACADEMIC LIBRARIES

The role of the library and information centre in a college is aimed at realizing the educational goals of the college or the parent organization. The college libraries not only provides stimulus to reading by procuring materials for study and research, by introducing open access system, by providing long hours of open, by organizing the library resources in a systematic way, but also feeds the intellect of the student, encourage the researches of the faculty and thus serve the teaching and research needs of the faculty. The college library and information resource centre acts as a vehicle for disseminating information and the related computer technologies through the best practices for utilization by its community of users and also for the exchange of information among its users (Umesh, 2012).

IMPACT OF ICT ON LIBRARY SERVICES

The global changes particularly in Information and Communication Technologies (ICT) have impact on the functioning of academic libraries. The developments in ICT have changed the users' expectation from the academic libraries in different ways. More than two decades ago there has been transforms from traditional access of information resources to online access to library catalogues, databases etc. in this context it indispensable for library to put up with the online services for users and provide access to – Online / Offline access to digital resources, Database searching, Electronic reference and library should have the facility online circulation service Information literacy program. There should be public relations services and conduct library promotion and marketing and also E-publishing (Sarasvathy, Manjunath, Giddaiah, & Mariswamy, 2014).

CHALLENGES FACED BY ACADEMIC LIBRARIES IN THE CHANGING ENVIRONMENT

1. Explosive growth of information and documents.
2. Focus on accountability - increasing demand for libraries to demonstrate outcomes / impacts in areas of importance to institution.
3. Increased cost of the documents and information materials.
4. Financial pressures - increasing pressure to maximize use of resources.
5. Increase in users information needs.
6. Emphasis on assessment of student performance / research out puts.
7. New role of the librarian and greater responsibilities.
8. Expectation for rapid document delivery.
9. User education in new technologies - latest techniques and concepts in handling of information.
10. New electronic information environment.
11. Creation of databases and its security.
12. Migration to online full-text sources.

13. Marketing of library and information services.
14. Greater need for staff training.

The library and information centre of an institution play a central role in facilitating dissemination and creation of new knowledge. In the present learning environment, the library and information centre as learning resource has taken up increasingly more academic space and time in the life of the user, thus it is time to identify and adopt the new ways that will lead library and information centre to improve their process and activities, thereby optimizing the resource utilization and delivering high quality, and value added services to their users (Umesh, 2012).

DEFINITION OF BEST PRACTICES

Best practices in the development of infrastructure and learning resources sustained practices leading to continuous improvement of infrastructure and learning resource development to create an optimum learning ambience. "A practice qualifies to a Best practice status if it resulted in high value impact on any aspect of educational activity in an institution". A best practice is a value added standard practice. However, a best practice may depend on viewer's perspective, time and context. Institutional excellence is the aggregate of the best practices followed in different areas of institutional activities. In general, the use of technology and innovative ideas lead to evolve best practices evolving in the library and information environment.

Online Dictionary of Library and Information Science (ODLIS) describes best practices as follows: "In the application of theory to real-life situations, procedures that, when properly, applied, consistently yield superior results and are therefore used as reference points in evaluation of the effectiveness of alternative methods of accomplishing the same task. Best practices are identified by examining empirical evidence of success." (Reitz, 2015).

Concise Oxford English Dictionary describes "Best practices as quality of most excellent or desirable type or most appropriate, advantageous, highly improved, outstanding, par excellence services or the customary or expected procedure or way of doing something that is usual or expected way in a particular organization or situation, guidelines for good practices. In this process of developing best practices we take action rather than good ideas, and we improve our skills" (Stevenson, & Waite, 2011).

Oxford Advanced Learners Dictionary describes "Best practices as quality of high standard, excellence, highly improved, outstanding, par excellence service. It means way of doing something that is usual or expected way in a particular organization or situation, guidelines for good practices. In this process of developing best practices it takes action rather than good ideas, and it improve the skills" (Deuter, Bradbery, & Turnbull, 2015).

Thus a 'Best practice' in library in simple terms is known as that practice which makes the way for enhancing an existing function or an activity and helps in effective implementation or use of the process thereby leading to a continuous improvement and overall performance of the library (NAAC, 2006). With this information as background an attempt has been made to highlight the practices that are adopted in the academic libraries.

NEED FOR BEST PRACTICES

A best practice is a practice which paves the way for enhancing an existing function and helps in effective implementation or use of the process. Use of technology in designing and delivering the information products and services in a library has always yielded good results. Automation of all in-house operations in academic libraries with bar-coding, user identity and web OPAC facilities is a best practice in totality of library services.

Effective implementation of user education/ awareness programs with the new techniques and tools will also be a best practice in extent of use of library services. Developing digital repositories with subject content, open sources and institutional information and customizing it to internal requirements with remote access is one of the globally adopted best practices in the university libraries. In the present era of IT, the academic libraries need to re-orient to the highly qualitative information collection and services (Sunitha, 2009). "Libraries are in the service business so it has to ensure quality in service. The most important product they have is service. Without service, libraries are indistinguishable from museums or they are a combination of a maze and morgue for books. Service is a pervasive ethic of the profession of librarianship" (Clayton, & Gorman, 2001; and Gorman, 2003).

DETERMINANTS OF SERVICE QUALITY

What is quality? It is customer satisfaction through product or service. In an academic library student and teachers are the customers who are part of the academic community. There are original ten general determinants / dimensions for evaluating of library service quality that can be applied to most types of service. These are general criteria that can be used to assess the quality of service customers expect and receive. These determinants can be used to formulate Best Practices (Sarasvathy, Manjunath, Giddaiah, & Mariswamy, 2014).

1. Access : the ease and convenience of accessing the service (s).

2. Communication : keeping your users informed; listening to your users.

3. Competence : having the skills and knowledge to provide the service (s).

4. Courtesy : politeness, respect, consideration, and friendliness of staff at all levels.

5. Credibility : trustworthiness, reputation and image.

6. Reliability : providing consistent, accurate and dependable service (s); delivering the service as promised.

7. Responsiveness : being willing and ready to provide service (s) when needed.

8. Security : physical safety; financial security; confidentiality.

9. Understanding the customer : knowing individual customer needs.

10. Tangibles : the physical aspects of the service such as equipment, facilities, resources.

Total Quality Management (TQM) stresses upon continuous improvement in services as core values. Peter Brophy compares libraries with automobile industry for the purpose of quality management. But according to S. Siraj Nissa Begum there is difference. She says "while in manufacturing concern, the customer is remote, where as in service organization like an academic library, producers and consumers meet face to face. Thus the complexity of managing service organizations is typically compounded by the existence of multiple interfaces" (Siraj Nissa Begum, Spring, 2003). Peter Brophy uses the following indicators for comparison: Performance, Features, Conformance, Reliability, Durability, Currency, Serviceability, Aesthetics, Perceived Quality, and Accessibility (Brophy, 2007).

Thus a library has to have a catalogue of stock, whether logically organized, is there full space and knowledgeable staff to help, is there any link to document delivery from the online catalogue, personal notification of new acquisitions, is there a coffee shop, libraries are following AACR, MARC, service standards (e.g., average acquisition time) are correct answers given to the queries, books of the library websites working properly, technology is durable despite user base is increasing, library acquires latest edition of books and journals, today's newspapers available when library opens, current CDROM mounted, corrections of errors in document supply, courtesy of staff, receptivity to complaints and suggestions, library building design including finishes, web home page design, library staff helpful and cooperative, OPACS are working well, Braille options is available as well as facilities for deaf. The above points if taken into account seriously which are part of the above attributes, it gives you some insights of 'quality' (Sivankalai, & Thulasi Kavitha Yadav, 2012).

NATIONAL ACCREDITATION AND ASSESSMENT COUNCIL (NAAC) AND BEST PRACTICES IN LIBRARY

University Grants Commission created a higher education body (whose job is to assess the quality of university and college institutions) in 1994 in Bangalore on the recommendation of National Policy of Education (NPE) in 1986. This is National Accreditation and Assessment Council (NAAC) which strives for quality and excellence in higher education and advocates for enhancing the role of library and Information Services in improving academic environment. NAAC prepared a document for "Best Practices in Academic Libraries (NAAC, 2006) says: Best practice may be innovative and be a philosophy, policy, strategy, program, process or practice that solves a problem or create new opportunities and positively impact on organizations." NAAC developed a set of best practices followed in academic libraries, classified and presented under the following four broad areas (Shrivastav, 2015):

1. Management and Administration of Library
    a. In-service Programmes
    b. Observation of other Library practice.
    c. Staff promotional policy.
    d. Maintenance of service area
    e. Special deposit scheme

f. Resource Generation through external membership.
g. Resource generation through internet services.
h. Student participation programme.

2. Collection and Services
   a. Collection development in different formats
   b. Compact storage of less used collection
   c. Library book exhibition
   d. Extended library opening hours
   e. Extended hours of service

3. Extent of User Services
   a. User education
   b. Initiation to freshers
   c. Preparatory course for students project
   d. User orientation
   e. Information aids
   f. Library use statistics
   g. Library best user award
   h. User feedback practice through different formats
   i. Suggestion box and timely response

4. Use of Technology in Libraries
   a. On-line information retrieval- Internet access
   b. Free browsing unit -Internet access.
   c. Broadband internet centre
   d. Library homepage for information dissemination
   e. A strong and dynamic library website
   f. User feedback through library homepage
   g. Access to e-resources
   h. Information retrieval through web OPAC

i. Campus-wide LAN facility

j. Database creation using international standard formats

k. Electronic surveillance system CCTV

College libraries need to have facilities that promote effective and interactive access and use of information resources for all users. In the area of physical facilities, the libraries need to offer safe, comfortable, well-lighted, clean space, with adequate and appropriate seating arrangements to ensure effective use of the library's resources including digital resources. Also, college libraries are required to consider study space needs, while allocating the seating space, with special attention being paid to reserve collections and the hostel environment of the institution. The libraries need to prepare well-framed rules and guidelines with regard to hours of access, circulation policies, and other regulations to offer better services to the users.

BEST PRACTICES FOR COLLEGE LIBRARIES

A database of documented practices is available on NAAC website and they assure that regular updating will be made with consultations on contributing institutions. For college libraries NAAC has developed the listed below are some of the best practices that can enhance the academic information environment and usability of college libraries.

1. Computerization of library with standard digital software.
2. Inclusion of sufficient information about the library in the college prospectus.
3. Compiling student / teacher attendance statistics and locating the same on the notice board.
4. Displaying newspaper clippings on the notice board and a clipping file maintained periodically.
5. Career / Employment Information / Services.

6. Internet Facilities to different user groups.
7. Information literacy programs.
8. Suggestion box and timely response.
9. Displaying new arrivals and circulating a list of those to academic departments.
10. Conducting book exhibitions on different occasions.
11. Organizing book talks.
12. Instituting Annual Best User Award for students.
13. Organizing competitions annually.
14. Conducting user surveys periodically.

However the above set of best practices for college libraries prepared by NAAC can not be termed as the last word. The following set of practices too should have been included in it.

1. Making of a Path Finder to the library
2. Keeping the library premises neat and clean
3. Compiling a list of Current Serials/ catalogue of journals.
4. Updating and maintaining library website
5. Maintaining useful statistics regarding the use of the library and displaying them on the library walls
6. Compiling checklists on different subject/topics as a part of documentation service
7. Library Committee formation
8. Distribution of useful handouts

The best practices all have mentioned might be in practice in many institutions. The outlined practices may serve as one of the ways to strengthen the library and information services of academic libraries (Umesh, 2012).

CASE STUDY: CHAKDAHA COLLEGE LIBRARY, CHAKDAHA, NADIA, WEST BENGAL

About the College

Foundation & Growth : Chakdaha College affiliated to the University of Kalyani was born on the 21st of November, 1972 in the cradle of suburban Bengal and has grown over the years into a leading and prestigious Under Graduate (UG) academy teaching Honors and General courses in Humanities, Science and Commerce subjects. By its academic discipline and a sustained record of toppers in almost all Honors courses it attracts and caters to the best budding talents of not only Chakdaha township but also of a vast hinterland that cuts across Nadia and other surrounding districts.

Achievement and Excellence : Over the years this college has been nurturing a blend of academic excellences and extracurricular achievements, high order of teaching and infrastructural development, in virtuoso. It is on record that the best of our alumni went abroad to enter the highest echelons of study and research, and a large part of them is now placed in teaching positions of higher education. The best athletes produced by this college won national acclaim and even Arjun Award. From the playground of this college, athletes (in handicapped section) were sent to international sports meet at Busan (South Korea) and Malaysia, and they won distinction there. Performance of the college has even attracted campus selection – a phenomenon not very characteristic of non professional academics. Alongside Honors and General Degree courses, UGC sponsored Remedial Coaching and Entry in Services for SC / ST / OBC / Minority students, UGC NRC, Career & Counselling are conducted on a regular basis. The college has been a Study Centre of Netaji Subhash Open University (NSOU) since 1998, a centre where UG and PG course in different subjects are conducted providing space for students who have dropped out of regular academic streams.

Ambience and Cultural : Activities In a serene landscape poster free walls and rooms provide an ideal ambience for study. Amenities like an auditorium, an open-air dais surrounding fields and an adjacent stadium beckon the students into the arena of sports and culture. Sports and socials apart, activities like internally resourced seminars, departmental publications, felicitations of the best performers in University examination and extra-curricula's, cultural festivals like: ANTORJATIK MATRI BHASA DIBAS and SHARAD UTSAB, inter-State cultural exchange programmes distinguish this college from its peers.

The College Building : The College has three separate and self-sufficient buildings for Arts, Commerce and Science faculties respectively on the sides of the central college ground. Each building is provided with well illuminated, spacious class-rooms, teachers' room and toilets. There are also separate administrative building, library and extension buildings inside the college campus.

Chakdaha College Library : The Chakdaha College Library is the intellectual hub of the Chakdaha College and provides a serene haven for those interested in pursuit of knowledge, in finding a quiet corner for their research and writing or even just catching up on the happenings of the day and the goings-on in the world through the newspapers and Internet. It is a place to read, surf, learn, disseminate and debate.

The Chakdaha College Library functions as the primary information resource centre, and repository of all printed for teaching and research activities at the institute. Apart from textbooks and recommended reading material prescribed for each course offered at the institute, the library houses a growing collection of research monographs, reports, multi-volume reference works, dictionaries, encyclopedias, handbooks, and so on. The library facilitates access to a number of journals through its participation in consortia, such as: N-LIST Programme. The library also subscribes to few journals directly from publishers as well as through reputed subscription agencies. At present, users can consult more than twenty five thousand five hundred (25500) books (available on shelves). The library is spacious (about 2500 square feet), well light, and well-ventilated. Its location allows for easy access and offers a seating capacity for 40 users.

Developing the library operations are automated using KOHA software, the Online Public Access Catalogue (OPAC) enables library users know their checkout status, issue history and Institutional Digital Repository (IDR) using DSpace is under way. This step will greatly enhance the library efficiency in making the resources available to the academic community at large and also enable the institute participate in various inter-library initiatives at national and international levels. Chakdaha College Library adopted NAAC developed set of best practices followed in academic libraries and worked under the following four broad areas and their respected best practices:

Best Practices of Chakdaha College Library

1. Preamble : Services of the Library are provided primarily to students, faculty, staff, and Office Bearers of the College, and are extended to member of public who satisfy certain terms and conditions. The library collections of the Chakdaha College are national property and as such are subject to special protection. These rules are designed to ensure that all members may obtain the maximum benefits from library facilities. All members should exercise self-discipline, respect and consideration for others when using the Library. By the act of using any facility of the Library, a user agrees to abide by these rules of the Library.

2. Scope : These rules and regulations govern the use of the Central Library, Project Collections, Special Collections and Statistical Workers' Circulating Library of the College. These rules supersede all existing rules and regulations of the Library.

3. Library Timings : The college library remains open to all college staff and students from 8.30 am to 5 pm on Monday, Wednesday and Friday; 10.30 am to 5 pm on Tuesday and Thursday and 10.30 am to 2 pm on Saturday.

4. Library Collection Development : The college library presently has more than 25,500 (Approx.) books. These include text books and rare costly reference books and up-dated information books.

5. The Chakdaha College Library is following a tradition of bifurcating of old edition and new edition books and housing in controlled and active stack area respectively for retrieval of new and old books by the users.

6. The college subscribes to journals, newspapers and periodicals. The following Newspapers / Magazines / Periodicals / Journals are available from Chakdaha College Library for the users (teaching, students and non teaching stuff) as reference service: a. 365 din; b. Bangla Statesman; c. Pratidin; d. The Statesman; e. The Competition Master; f. Karma Khetra; g. Safolya; h. Karma Sansthan; i. Khela; j. Employment News; k. Science Reporter; l. desh; m. Pesha Prabesh; n. Economic & Political Weekly (EPW); o. Saptahik Bartaman; p. Resonance: journal of science education (ISSN: 0971-8044); q. Indian Journal of Political Science (ISSN: 0019-5510).

7. Newspapers and Periodicals are issued against Library cards for Reading in the library. Journals will be issued for current reading in the library only.

8. Infrastructures : There is 1 workstation at the first floor and in addition to these upcoming workstations with 6 computers for users to access e-resources with reading hall facility.

9. Authorities, etc. : In view of the decision of the Governing Body (GB) all the obsolete books of the H. S. course and old pattern degree course are to be disposed off and sold through the Library Sub Committee (LSC) and amount of money collected through process are to be utilized for purchasing the books for the college library.

10. Library Card : Every student must possess his / her Library Card while making use of the Library facility and produce the same to the Library Staff on entering the Library.

11. Membership card is nontransferable. Students must not lend their Library Card to any other student to borrow books from the Library. Library facilities will be withdrawn for students misusing cards.

12. First year students should get their Library Card issued from the library by the prescribed date. No Library Card will be issued to any student after this date. However, only in special cases or under genuine circumstances the Library Card will be issued to the students after obtaining the Principal's permission.

13. Library Card must be renewed every year as notified.

14. Discipline : Strict discipline must be maintained in the Library. Disregard of library rules, indiscipline and misbehavior may lead to disciplinary action and access to the library privileges may be withdrawn.

15. Reference material should not be taken outside the Library.

16. Extension Services : The Chakdaha College Library is encouraging youngsters to compete in competitive exams like: IAS, ICS, WBCS, Staff Selection Commission, CAT, MAT, GATE, etc. by providing competitive exam books housed at reference section.

17. Books for overnight reading will be issued at specific time as decided by the Librarian and the same must be returned before 9.30 AM next day.

18. Book Manuals : The students may consult the library book manuals for respective departmental books and check which books are there for use.

19. Reading : Students are allowed to use reading room for reading purposes on submission of their reading cards.

20. Borrowing / Lending Section : Each student is provided with a lending Card (two for Honors and one for General students) for borrowing books. Books can be borrowed for a period of 7 days. A fine of fifty paisa per day will be charged if books not submitted within due date.

21. Each full time teachers fifteen (15) books, part time teachers and non teaching staff ten (10) books can borrow for sixty (60) days and guest teachers three (3) books can borrow for thirty (30) days from the date of issuing from the library at a time respectively.

22. Maximum two extensions (renewed) of the period of loan for another fifteen days is possible if the book is brought to the library or the request is communicated through personal visit / telephone / e-mail, prior to the due date of return, provided there is no demand for the issued item from other members before or on the due date stamped. After two extensions the book has to be returned to the library and cannot be renewed for a third time.

23. If library card is lost duplicate card will be issued on submission of Rs. 20/- (Reference card) and Rs. 20/- (lending card).

24. The teaching and non teaching staff who will be retiring shortly must have to return the library books before one (1) month of the retirement. The library staff will convey the concerned teaching and non teaching staff regarding the books lending in his / her name before three (3) months of his / her retirement.

25. Periodicals : Members can borrow three back issues of select periodicals for a period of fifteen days. Two extensions of the period of loan for another fifteen days is possible if the book / periodical is brought to the library or the request is communicated through personal visit / telephone / e-mail, prior to the due date of return, provided there is no demand for the issued item from other members before or on the due date stamped. After two extensions the book / periodical has to be returned to the library and cannot be renewed for a third time.

26. Care of Books / Periodicals : Once a book / periodical are issued it is wholly the responsibility of the member to safeguard and return the issued materials to library in good condition and on time. Before borrowing book (s) / periodical (s), members are encouraged to check that the book (s) / periodical (s) are in proper condition. If they are found to be mutilated or damaged on return, the member will be held responsible for the damage and (s) he will have to replace or pay the price of the damaged book / periodical. The library reserves the right to determine the price of a rare / out-of-print / unobtainable book / periodical.

27. Loss or Damage : Students are required to handle books and reading material very carefully. Marking library books with pencil or ink, tearing the pages or spoiling the same in any other way will be viewed very seriously. In such case, the last reader will be held responsible unless he shows the Librarian at the time of issue that the book had been previously marked or damaged. In the event of damage of any kind, the last reader will be liable to compensate for damage. Books will have to be replaced.

28. If a member loses or damages any book that (s) he has borrowed, it will have to be replaced by a new copy of the same or later edition at his / her cost. In the event of the book not being available or out of print in the market then similar type of books of the same standard should be returned, otherwise the published price of the book will have to be reimbursed to the library. No specimen copy in lieu of the lost book can be accepted by the library.

29. If a member loses or damages any periodical that (s) he has borrowed, it will have to be replaced by a new copy of the same at his / her cost. In the event of the periodical issue not being available, the published price of the particular issue will have to be reimbursed to the library.

30. In case of Indian publication, the amount to be paid for a lost book will be double the original price and in case of foreign publication, the amount to be paid will be three times the original price of the lost book.

31. Library Clearance : The College Leaving Certificate or Transfer Certificate will be issued to student only after he / she has returned all the Library books and cleared all library dues.

32. Future plans : The College has already made computer catalogues for all the books in the library for students' ready-use.

33. The college plans to install computers in the library so that a student may trace the status of a book whether that is available in the library or borrowed by someone else, how many copies of that book the library has etc, by a click of the mouse.

34. It is observed that some of the students do not return the Library Books on or before the due date stamped on the date slip attached in the book depriving other students.

35. In order to prevent such students from keeping Library books with them beyond due date, the fine charged will be as follows:

- First week after the due date: Rs. 10/- per day
- For second week after the due date: Rs. 20/- per day
- Beyond 15 days, the borrower will have to pay the cost of the book along with fine.

36. Planning to setting up with 2 workstations and reading hall.

37. To assess the use pattern of Chakdaha College Library web OPAC (like time of access, discipline, designation, duration, etc.). The authority is planning to assign an individual user ID login and password.

38. Chakdaha College Library authority is planning to provide e-books facility for negotiates further purchase / collection.

39. Chakdaha College Library is setting up to Digital Library of holdings.

40. Chakdaha College Library is planning to create bibliographic details for Publications of Chakdaha College Journals / Publications like: college workshops, seminars and conference proceedings, etc.

CONCLUSION

The academic libraries should take initiations of the broad activity to enhance the socio-economic position of the books / documents in the library. Also they should create an environment and conditions for keeping abreast of the new and latest knowledge and uses of modern technological achievements in the field, and also in the diffusion of the latest information and lastly the training of professional personnel through a unified system, so that the knowledge from the source to its beneficiaries or users can be disseminated in a most efficient and effective way through the adoption of the best practices (Umesh, 2012).

The concept of survival of the fittest of Charles Darwin's ideas of evolution through natural selection, is very much applicable here, immediately if library professional does not come up with technology and update their knowledge and skill to render library service, collection of resources. As the Computer and Management researchers and scientist are occupying the area of Information science, Technology, and Management it is a high time for library professionals to be alert and update the ICT skills and implement Best practice to survive (Sarasvathy, Manjunath, Giddaiah, & Mariswamy, 2014).

In accordance with NAAC standards, libraries should establish, promote, maintain, and evaluate a range of quality services that support the colleges, mission and goals (Waghmode, 2013). To cope with the timely challenges, every library has to identify and develop its own tailor-made best practices to enhance the collection development process, services dissemination and use of the library as a whole. Appropriate planning, fore thinking, a detailed analysis of user base, objectives of the affiliating institution and its future strategies should be taken into account while planning any best practice. Many library stakeholders grumble that any best practice means involvement of a lot of resources especially in terms of money and equipments. In fact it requires active participation, willingness, creativity and problem solving attitude from the library stakeholders. Developing best practices, analyzing and revising them at a regular interval will lead to continuous improvement in overall performance of the library and the whole institution (Kamble, & Tikam, 2010).

Thus the best practices adopted should bridge the gap between the library and the users for effective and maximum utilization of the resources, which will result in the advancement and promotion of higher educational goals and the vision and mission of the library. The best practices are evolved through stages of failures and corrections and through the borrowed best practices we can enhance our competitive advantage and also enhance the institutional effectiveness (Umesh, 2012).

In the process of achieving best practices in libraries, Prof. A. C. Tikekar warns us "Blind imitation, false competition and status symbolism do not work well. Adhocism too does not accomplish the desired goal. Planned radical change would prove costly and unwieldy. At the same time both resistance and or reluctance to accept the inevitable changes will be harmful to development of libraries" (Tikekar, 2009). It is suggested that there are areas which we have not been able to find out as best practices. A few examples of such areas are: index to periodicals, real time reference service, preparation of various statistics of the use of e-resources and many other areas.

In this paper confined that as per NAAC guidelines Chakdaha College Library adopted various best practices in its administration, management, collection and services, Extent of the Use of Services and use of technology. Chakdaha College Library implemented the Information literacy and user awareness programs with normative practices through best practices. In its effective implementation that make significant change in enhancing the use of information sources / services and users satisfaction level. The documentation on the best practices followed in the Chakdaha College Library will initiate other libraries to opt for the ideal way of managing the libraries and services of academic institutions. In all, concerned areas of library, services and users, Chakdaha College Library worked with full concentration.

REFERENCES

1. Ahemad, Merina., & Pal, Birender. (2012). Best practices with NAAC in college libraries of Nalbari District, Assam. In

proceedings of the 8th Convention on Promotion of Library Automation and Networking in North Eastern Region (PLANNER 2012), Sikkim University, Gangtok, March 1-3, 2012 (pp. 379-386). Ahmedabad: INFLIBNET Centre. Retrieved March 6, 2015, from http://ir.inflibnet.ac.in/bitstream/1944/1705/1/47.pdf.

2. Brophy, Peter. (2007). The library in the twenty-first century: new services for the information age. 2nd rev.ed. London: Facet.

3. Choudaha, Rahul. (August, 2013). Statistics on Indian higher education: 2012-2013. In Dr. Education: International Higher Education Blog: trends, insights and strategies on internationalization of higher education. Retrieved March 4, 2015, from http://www.dreducation.com/2013/08/data-statistics-india-student-college.html.

4. Clayton, Peter and Gorman, G. E. (2001). Managing information resources in libraries: collection management in theory and practice. London: Library Association.

5. Deuter, Margaret., Bradbery, Jennifer., & Turnbull, Joanna. (2015). Oxford advanced learner's dictionary. New 9th Ed. London: Oxford University Press.

6. Gorman, Michael. (2003). The enduring library: technology, tradition and the quest for balance. Chicago; London: American Library Association.

7. India Education. (December, 2014). Universities in India. In India Education: Gyaan at every step. Retrieved March 5, 2015, from http://www.indiaeducation.net/universities/.

8. Kamble, Ajay., & Tikam, Madhuri V. (2010). Best practices in academic libraries. *Best Practices in Academic Libraries - LIS Compendium,* 1-8. Retrieved February 21, 2015, from https://liscompendium.wordpress.com/; https://liscompendium.wordpress.com/article/best-practices-in-academic-libraries-35muq6i9t1aro-3/.

9. Mahajan, Preeti. (2005). Academic libraries in India: a present-day scenario. *Library Philosophy and Practice (e-journal),* 8 (1), Paper 66, 1-4. Retrieved February 24, 2015, from http://digitalcommons.unl.edu/libphilprac/66/;

10. National Assessment and Accreditation Council (NAAC). (2006). Best practices in library and information services: a case presentations. Bangalore: NAAC. Retrieved March 8,

2015, from www.naac.gov.in/docs/Best%20Practices%20in%20%20Library%20and%20Information%20Services%20A%20Case%20Presentation.doc.

11. National Assessment and Accreditation Council (NAAC). (2006). Guidelines on quality indicators in library and information services: affiliated / constituent colleges. Bangalore: NAAC. Retrieved March 9, 2015, from http://www.naac.gov.in/docs/Guidelines-Colleges-Library.pdf.

12. Reitz, Joan M. (2015). Online Dictionary for Library and Information Science (ODLIS). CA: ABC-CLIO, LLC. Retrieved March 7, 2015, from http://www.abc-clio.com/ODLIS/odlis_b.aspx.

13. Sarasvathy, P., Manjunath, M., Giddaiah, D., & Mariswamy, C. (2014). Best practices of Mysore University Library: an overview. In *Changing Faces of Libraries in Digital Era*, March 6-7, 2014 (pp. 1-7). Karnataka State Women's University, Bijapur. Bijapur: Karnataka State Women's University. Retrieved March 2, 2015, from http://eprints.uni-mysore.ac.in/16673/; http://eprints.uni-mysore.ac.in/view/subjects/ICA-LI.html; http://eprints.uni-mysore.ac.in/16673/1/Best%20practices%20of%20Mysore%20University%20Library%20An%20Overview.pdf.

14. Shrivastav, Shail. (2015). Best practices in academic library. *Research Link: An International, Registered & Referred Monthly Journal - 132*, 14 (1), 147-148. Retrieved March 10, 2015, from http://www.researchlink.in/FullIssue/Research%20Link%20132/19%20Library%20Science.pdf.

15. Siraj Nissa Begum, S. (Spring, 2003). Total quality management in the academic library. *Library Philosophy and Practice*, 5 (2), 1-3. Retrieved March 11, 2015, from http://digitalcommons.unl.edu/libphilprac/3; http://www.webpages.uidaho.edu/~mbolin/begum-tqm.pdf.

16. Sivankalai, S., & Thulasi Kavitha Yadav, S. (2012). Total quality management in academic libraries: a study. *International Journal of Educational Research and Technology*, 3 (1), 66-72. Retrieved March 11, 2015, from http://soeagra.com/ijert/ijert_march2012/11.pdf.

17. Stevenson, Angus., & Waite, Maurice. (Ed.) (2011). Concise Oxford English Dictionary. 12th ed. United Kingdom, New Delhi: Oxford University Press.

18. Sunitha, K. H. (2009). Effective practices to enhance skills at the Learning Resource Centers. In *Proceedings of International Conference on Academic Libraries (ICAL - 2009): Technology, Policy and Innovation, Change Management, Library - Publisher / Vendor Interface, Management Models and Framework, Library Services, Advocacy,* University of Delhi (North Campus), Delhi University Library System, Delhi, India, October 5-8, 2009 (pp. 361-370). Delhi: Delhi University Library System, University of Delhi (North Campus). Retrieved March 3, 2015, from http://crl.du.ac.in/ical09/papers/index_files/ical-61_217_462_1_RV.pdf.

19. Tikekar, A. C. (2009). Best practices in academic libraries. Paper presented at the program "Vision Libraries - 2020" A One Day Saminar for College Librarians, organized by Central Library, North Maharastra University, Jalgaon, April 8, 2009. Jalgaon: North Maharastra University.

20. Tikekar, A. C. (2009). Towards 21st century academic libraries and librarianship. In *Proceedings of International Conference on Academic Libraries (ICAL - 2009): Technology, Policy and Innovation, Change Management, Library - Publisher / Vendor Interface, Management Models and Framework, Library Services, Advocacy,* Delhi University Library System, University of Delhi (North Campus), Delhi, India, October 5-8, 2009 (pp. 45-50). Delhi: Delhi University Library System, University of Delhi (North Campus). Retrieved March 10, 2015, from http://crl.du.ac.in/ical09/papers/index_files/ical-8_235_527_1_RV.pdf.

21. Umesh, K. Y. (2012). Best practices adopted in academic libraries and information resource centres. *International Journal of Information Dissemination and Technology,* 2 (3), 186-188. Retrieved February 23, 2015, from http://www.ijidt.com/index.php/ijidt/article/view/198/91.

22. University Grants Commission (UGC). (2013). Annual report: 2012-2013. New Delhi: University Grants Commission. Retrieved February 27, 2015, from http://www.ugc.ac.in/pdfnews/6022729_English-Report-2012-13.pdf.

23. University Grants Commission (UGC). (June, 2013). Higher education in India at a glance. New Delhi: University Grants Commission. Retrieved February 26, 2015, from http://www.ugc.ac.in/pdfnews/6805988_HEglance2013.pdf.

24. University Grants Commission (UGC). (September, 2013).

University development in India basic facts and figures, examination results: 2010 (annual & supplementary). New Delhi: Information & Statistics Bureau, University Grants Commission. Retrieved February 28, 2015, from http://www.ugc.ac.in/pdfnews/2519852_UDI10.pdf.

25. Vyas, S. D. (2009). Best practices in academic libraries in India: a study. In *Proceedings of International Conference on Academic Libraries (ICAL - 2009): Technology, Policy and Innovation, Change Management, Library - Publisher / Vendor Interface, Management Models and Framework, Library Services, Advocacy,* Delhi University Library System, University of Delhi (North Campus), Delhi, India, October 5-8, 2009 (pp. 418-421). Delhi: Delhi University Library System, University of Delhi (North Campus). Retrieved February 25, 2015, from http://crl.du.ac.in/ical09/papers/index_files/ical-71_149_326_1_RV.pdf.

26. Wadje, Kailas N. (2012). Best practices in library of Indira Gandhi Senior College (IGSC), Nanded. *Research Vistas: The Ultimate Destination for Researchers,* 1 (2) [March-April, 2012], 97-107. Retrieved February 22, 2015, from http://www.researchvistas.com/rvvol1issue2.htm; http://egranthalaya.nic.in/16Kailas.pdf.

27. Waghmode, Shahaji Shankar. (2013). *Best practices in Sonubhau Baswant College Library: a study.* In *UGC Sponsored National Conference on Changing Paradigm of Academic Libraries in the E-Environment,* Ulhasnagar, January 7-8, 2013 (pp. 1-8). Ulhasnagar. Retrieved March 1, 2015, from http://eprints.rclis.org/22785/1/EPRINT%20Best%20Practices%20in%20SBCLibrary%20Shahapur.pdf.

20

Best Practices in Shri M. D. Shah Mahila College of Arts and Commerce, College Library, Malad, Mumbai

Vinay P. Haware
Librarian, Shri. M.D.Shah Mahila College of Arts & Commerce, B.J.Patel Road, Malad (W) Mumbai 64

ABSTRACT

Shri M.D.Shah Mahila College of Arts and Commerce, Malad (W) Mumbai is among the affiliated colleges of the SNDT Women's University. 45 yr old institution serves for the 3000 degree and 6000 junior college women students. The College Library making efforts to attract the students to the library as they are distancing from this heart of the institution. Various practices are followed by the Library to make students comfort to their study not only related to their curriculum but also seeding the upcoming readers for the society. Undergraduate students are observed very reluctant to the reading and distancing from the variety of general reading. Library makes some positive efforts to inculcate the reading habits among these students as well as making them comfort to the modern technology too by the procurement of e-reading materials. The paper will highlight the efforts of the library in last decade to attract these students which brought the students closer to reading.

INTRODUCTION

The academic library has been from its inception an integral part of institutions of higher Learning, rather than an appendix or adjunct. The academic library, like any other formal establishment, is designed and run people whose job is to combine and use organizational resources to achieve organizational objectives. The term administration is used to identify this group of people.

Over the past 25 years, academic libraries have been affected by changes in information technology. The rate of change is still accelerating in this area. The introduction of various Information Technology (IT) trends has led to reorganizations, changes in work patterns, and demand for new skills, job retraining, and reclassification of positions. The technological development of the past 25 years, such as the electronic database, online services, CD-ROMs, and the introduction of Internet has radically transformed access to information.

LIBRARIANSHIP

The perennial duty of the librarian as midwife to the birth of knowledge has not changed appreciably with the passing of centuries. If anything there has been increased recognition of our responsibilities for preserving cultural heritages in an age of virtuality and transience. Our procedures and materials have been found and lost and found again, invented and re-invented, named and re-named, as have our titles changed repeatedly. But the tradition of the librarian as a critical mediator in the flow of knowledge between creators and clients of tablets, scrolls, manuscripts, books, documents, recordings, pages and files has endured. Within the automated architectures of proliferating technology we are sought after for our intellectual methods and communication model. With the global maturation of our professional associations comes our responsiveness and effectiveness. We have expanded our introspective awareness into an overview of this efficacy, becoming reflective about our tradition of meta-scholarship conducted in collaborative effort.

Librarianship, predating both documentation and computing as specific disciplines, has not surprisingly previously realized episodes of crises of its identity.

LIBRARY NEEDS IN DEVELOPING COUNTRIES

Six characteristics of American librarianship are worthy of export:

1. The conception of the library as an organization of books and reading material.
2. The evolution of a library profession.
3. The attitude of service
4. The function of the library as an education institution,
5. The role of the library in the advancement of intellectual freedom, and
6. The conception of organized information as a public resource and responsibility.

LIBRARIANSHIP IN DEVELOPING COUNTRIES

Closed shelves, lack of extensive reference or circulating services, differing or absence of classification schemes, limited service and, above all, an emphasis on the primacy of the book over the reader are characteristics of Third World libraries. These characteristics are still prevalent today.

In recent years, certain social administrative and psychological forces make it mandatory for information professions in general and librarian in particular to acquire skills in technology, marketing and entrepreneurship or become irrelevant in the 21st century science and technologically driven information society. In this period of constant change, library managers should know that they are in the business of communicating.

They are responsible for management of ideas, beliefs, and information. Traditionally there are two components within the administrative structure of the academic library. The first is the collated information, i.e., in written, printed and electronic format. The other component is the intellectual tool set: the skills such as cataloguing, indexing, and reference work.

AWARENESS ABOUT IPR

The academic environment is full of activities by the students. They are doing various projects within their curriculum. Most of the time they are using references but many of them are least aware of the IPR. It is very much necessary to tell them about the copyright issues. The tangible medium requirement expands copyright from traditional writings and pictures into the realm of video, sound recordings, computer disks, and internet communications (Crews, 2009).

Name of the practice

Attracting the Under Graduate students to the Library

Goal of the Practice

In places where the college libraries are supposed to be the most important unit in the formal education, number of students visiting the college Library is decreased. The Librarian has to attract the students towards the library. In other words the students are distancing from the library. Through surveys, it was observed that the students of commerce faculty refer very rarely to library books. As the college has 40% students of commerce such a practice is essential. College library applied such policies that the number of students visiting to the library increased and the increased rate of issuing of books effectively observed.

THE POLICIES: FIRST PHASE

1. Attractive counter and entrance of the library. Addition of new attractive furniture.

2. Good looking colour cards for library users.
3. Addition of CD-ROM's, Vic's, video & audio material.
4. Separate reference section, ventilated, better arranged reading room.
5. Addition of latest reference sources.
6. Free internet access.
7. Computerized catalogue, along with the card catalogues.
8. Career guidance for l.i.s. Studies.
9. Open access system.
10. Recommendation of students to other libraries.
11. Implementing the ideas from the students.
12. Helping students in their project work. Restoring of question papers and syllabi.
13. Data entry by the students appointed as trainees.
14. Helping students in their project work.
15. Book exhibitions and seminar.
16. Orientation
17. Healthy personal relations with students.

EFFECTIVENESS OF THE PRACTICE IN FIRST PHASE

It is observed that the students visit the library on alternate days for routine enquiries related to their studies and also another purpose. Holding the new attractive card makes them feel comfortable and fashionable in comparison than older one. Students visit for internet use. They prefer library than going to cyber café. And finally looking at the books in the racks, they develop an urge to read.

THE POLICIES: SECOND PHASE

1. New wider LCD computers for good display and pleasure.
2. Broadband internet connection for high speed.

3. Digital information access from data bases based on personal I.D.
4. E-books and e-journals subscription.
5. Online Database of old question papers.
6. Online catalogue. (OPAC)
7. Identity card with barcode. One 'All' purpose card.
8. No separate Library card.
9. Fully automated transaction of books by using SOUL software.
10. N-List program membership.
11. Linkages to the other institutions.
12. Orientation using ICT Aids to more comfortable understandings.
13. Visual representation of the library on the web of outreaching up to users.
14. Attractive and innovative signage and notice board with suggestion box.

EFFECTIVENESS OF THE PRACTICE IN SECOND PHASE

It is observed that the students are more comfortable with the digital material to books for the references. By providing new fast computer with wider LCD screens students were happy to use Library. At the same time orientation about the information literacy help them to find out the correct and authentic information. Also students turn to printed book for the information as they were alert about the authentication of the information on the internet.

Key Finding

Students are seeking staff interaction to serve their needs. Staff must be available and willing to help.

Diversify material types to meet more user needs. Users short on time may prefer a movie to a book, and those with commutes may prefer audio books as opposed to print.

If Users are browsing materials, collections must be browsable. It's easier to change to fit Users needs than it is to retrain them. Communicate sections in common language instead of solely relying on call numbers to guide browsing.

Users are utilizing the library as meeting and study space, not just for items, computers or services. Allotting space for study and socializing needs is important when creating an overall atmosphere of service.

REFERENCES

- Crews, k. D. (2009). Copyright Low for Librarians and Educators(p. 5). New Delhi: Indiana Publishing House.

Other references

- Aggarwal B. S. : *An Introduction to Library and Information Science*, ABD, Delhi, 2005.
- Ajay K. : *Digital Library Environment and Networking*, Sree Pub, Delhi, 2006.
- Ali Amjad : *Ane's Encyclopedic Dictionary of Library and Information Science*, Ane Books India, Delhi, 2006.
- Aswal R.S. : *Library Automation for 21 Century*, Ess Ess Pub, Delhi, 2006.
- Ballabh Anand : *Library Classification and Cataloguing : Modern Concepts and Practices*, Akansha, Delhi, 2010.
- Bruce E : *The Practical Library Manager*, Ane Books India, Delhi, 2006.
- Danton, J. Periam: *The Dimensions of Comparative Librarianship*, Chicago, American Library Association, 1973.
- Devarajan G. : *Applied Research in Library and Information Science*, Ess Ess Pub, Delhi, 2005.
- Godia Kundan : *Electronic Services in Library and Information Science*, Adhyayan, Delhi, 2007.
- Hugh A. : *Internet Resources : A Subject Guide*, Chicago: Association of College and Research Libraries, 1995.
- Iyenger V.K. : *Digital Library Use : Librarian's Guide to Internet*, Arise Pub, Delhi, 2011.
- Joteen R.K. : *Information and Library Network Programme in 21st Century*, B.R. Pub, Delhi, 2010.

- Lancaster F. W. : *Intelligent Technologies : In Library and Information Service Applications,* Ess Ess Pub, Delhi, 2009.
- Lawrence A. : *The Librarian's Guide to Microcomputer Technology and Applications,* NY: Knowledge Industry Publications, 1983.
- Michael R. : *Collection Development and Collection Evaluation: A Source book,* Metuchen, NJ: Scarecrow Press, 1995.
- Ross Harvey : *Preservtion in Libraries: Principles, Strategies and Practices for Librarians,* London: Bowker-Saur, 1993.
- Sahib Singh *: Library and Literacy Movement for National Development,* Concept, Delhi, 2003.
- Sharma, Lokesh *: Library Management : An Organisational Perspective,* Shri Sai Printographers, Delhi, 2003.
- Singh Mahender Pratap *: Use of Information Technology in Library and Information Science,* Abhijeet, Delhi, 2004.

21

Open Study Centre as A Best Practices at Mss's, Arts, Science and Commerce College Library, Ambad, Jalna

Shivshankar Ghumre
Librarian, MSS's, Arts, Science and Commerce College, Ambad Dist. Jalna

ABSTRACT

The present paper highlights on the Open Study Centre as a best practices used at MSS's Arts, Science and Commerce College.

Keywords: Best Practices, Libraries, Open Study Centre.

INTRODUCTION

The higher and professional education is moving more and more towards privatization. Educational Institutions no longer wish to make their budget requirements a liability on their national exchequer, but on the country are trying to mobilize their own resources to provide better services, by following best practices. The libraries in this regard have become part of this strategy and the parent organization are investing sizable sum of development of libraries to improve services with better infrastructure.

Goals of the Practice : Following are the objective of the undertaking:

i) Utilizing the spare time of students for an academic cause;

ii) Using the occasion to create studies interest among them;

iii) Helping the college maintain discipline;

The Jalna district is a backward district in respect of economic development, health facilities, irrigation management, and social status compared to other district of Maharashtra state. Jalna district declared as educationally backward by the UGC and also one of the district having lowest human development index. Matsyodari Shikshan Sanstha's Arts and Commerce College, Ambad has been working in comprehensively so backward a district since 1979. The number of educating pupils of the college counts 3300. All the students come from rural area and are the "first educating generation".

It was a big challenge to serve at a standard level as a librarian in such a rural scenario. The measurement of library building of the college is 12000 is sq.feet. The library is systematic and inclusive of all facilities. Using the SOUL2.0 software, the library has been computerized. The library consist of individual facilities like Circulation section, Reference section, periodical section, Reprography section, and Audio - Visual section. The UGC funded/ sponsored Network Resource Centre is established with 25 PCs having broad band connectivity. The library have rich collection of books, journals and having huge access of e-resources (such as Science Direct | Springer Journals & Books | IEEE/IEE | ACM | Taylor & Francis | EBSCO | American Chemical Society | American Institute of Physics | American Physical Society | Annual Reviews | Cambridge University Press| Economic & Political Weekly | Emerald | Institute of Physics | JSTOR | Oxford Journals | Project Muse |

Royal Society of Chemistry | ScienceDirect (10 Subject Collection) | SpringerLink | Web of Science | J-Gate | ISID | JCCC | Wiley Online Library | Royal Society of Chemistry | ProQuest Dissertations & Theses A&I | ProQuest ABI/INFORM Complete | World Scientific Journals | Indian Journals | EBSCO Journals | eJurix Indias Electronic Law Library |

World E-Book Library | IEEE CS |) There are separate reading section for the student and the staff. The reading room of student bears a seating capacity of hundred. The reading room has been open for student between 9.30a.m. and 11.00 p.m. Despite all these facilities some student were discovered roaming about in the campus ; it was seriously thought over. And after researching nature of the problem one solution came out in the from of establishment of the Open Study Centre.

Despite the fact that there had been a reading room of 3000 sq.feet, network resource centre of about 1000 sq. ft. in the library, there was a special insight for creation of the open study center. The students were wasting the spare lectures and recess wandering here and there and discussing uselessly while some other got bored sitting in the library. Therefore, it was necessary to utilize their time for a proper purpose. It was significant to properly direct their caliber and induce them with reading culture. That is why the undertaking was implemented apace. College constructed and implemented separate open study centers for boys and girls.

As the Open Study Centers are close to the library, the students can avail themselves of facilities like reading newspaper, periodicals and books. The facility of light is already available there. As a result the student prefer sitting in the open space of the centre to sitting in the library enjoying themselves. Also, the Reading Room of the library has been a funhouse, with the reading public. The Open Study Centers comprises a nice arrangement of seats which also adds to pleasure of the studious students in the natural atmosphere. The centres has restrains mischievousness of the students. The Open Study Center reminds one of Tagore's original Shantiniketan.

Outcome of the Practice : At the left of the collegiate library a land for 3000 sq.ft. and infront of the library about 5000 sq.ft land was developed with a protective parapet wall for 3 feet for girl and boy students respectively. The trees of Neem, Karanji, Nilgiri have been planted around under the shade of which a permanent arrangement of seating 70 girl and 150 boy students has been made. All the construction and campus development work has been carried out under "Earn and Learn" scheme of the college. The students continuously keep studying in such a natural ambience.

THE BENEFITS OF OPEN STUDY CENTERS

The library experienced following benefits of the open study centers.

1) Students could be practiced to reading.
2) Reading room breathed a sigh of relief; the casual readers sat reading in the Open Study Center.
3) The number of student behaving purposelessly, being mischievous and wasting their time reduced.
4) Used to sitting in the center, the student avoided wandering through veranda and campus which ultimately helped maintain discipline.

Resources required for implementing the practice : The Open Study Center is set up on a free space akin to the library.

The setting up task was carried out under the "Earn and Learn" scheme run by the college which curtailed maximum of expenses. The centre is surrounded by the wall of three feet height upon which there are iron grills about two feet tall. The internal space is clean and beauteous. The trees are planted under the dark shade of which the students study. The availability of light encourages student to study at night. The students working under "Earn and learn" scheme offered their comprehensive labours that saved the following capital;

1) Building material and the skilled masons.
2) The shade of trees, cultivators of the trees, beautifying vines, flowers, plants, etc.
3) Vision to implement so an undertaking.

Open study centre is one of the best practices of the library. While library is working in backward district like Jalna and facing problems like man, money and technology, library tries to serve the best with help of such practices.

22

Best Practices in Academic Libraries Prescribed by NAAC

Shilpa Satish Waghchour

Librarian, Gokhale Education Society'

College of Education and Research, Parel, Mumba

INTRODUCTION

In the accreditation process, evaluation of librarie is an essential component, where the collection, service and their outreaching capacity are monitored. In th recent past, significant developments have been reporte in library and information services and the libraries ar shouldering newer responsibilities in higher educatio Hence the standards for assessing the quality of librar services need to be updated. It is true that libraries large support learning, teaching and research processes i institutions. So far, the classroom has, by and large, bee the primary source of learning, with library accorded supplementary status. In times ahead, one can foresee role reversal, and indeed, in the increasingly learne centric educational effort, one may already be witness the library becoming the primary learning resource many instances, with conventional classroom teachi playing mainly facilitating role. The paper compiles t Best Practices in Academic Libraries prescribed by NAA

Best Practices suggested by NAAC

1. Observation of other library practices by institutional visits
2. In-service program
3. Maintenance of service areas
4. Resource generation (through external membership)
5. Student internship programme
6. Student participative programme
7. Earn while learn programme
8. Library science as optional course/paper
9. Compact storage of less used collection
10. Collection development in different formats
11. Library book exhibition
12. Extended library opening hours
13. Collection enhancement in hybrid library
14. Initiation to fresher (Information Literacy Program)
15. User Education (Information literacy programme)
16. Preparatory course for students' projects (Information literacy programme)
17. User orientation (Information literacy programme)
18. Information aids (Information literacy programme)
19. Information aids (Information literacy programme)
20. Library use statistics
21. Library use statistics
22. Library best user award
23. User feedback practice through different formats.
24. User Feedback Practice thru suggestion boxes
25. On-line information retrieval (Internet access facility)
26. Free browsing Unit (Internet access facility)
27. Broad band Internet Center (Internet access facility)
28. Library homepage for Information dissemination

29. Dynamic Library Website
30. User feedback through library homepage
31. 24/7 Access to e-resources
32. Group concessional Night Services offer for outside students and scholars in accessing e-resources.
33. Access to Digital repository through library website.
34. Digital access to all internal documents
35. Digital repositories
36. CD NET server facility
37. Digitization of manuscripts
38. Multi lingual, integrated, web enabled database with complete automation of in-house services
39. Using self developed integrated Library software (Automation of in-house services)
40. Web OPAC
41. Information retrieval through Web OPAC
42. Campus-wide local area network (LAN) facility
43. Database creation using international standard formats
44. Electronic surveillance system

CONCLUSION

The best practices outlined in the document will be reviewed periodically and the up to date policies and practices will be framed. We do hope that this basic document would initiate the best practices in the Indian academic libraries.

REFERENCE

http://www.naac.gov.in/best_practices.asp